DISCOVER THE INDIAN SUBCONTINENT

Reader's Digest

PUBLISHED BY THE READER'S DIGEST ASSOCIATION LIMITED

LONDON   NEW YORK   SYDNEY   MONTREAL

DISCOVER THE INDIAN SUBCONTINENT
Translated and edited by Toucan Books Limited, London
for Reader's Digest, London

Translated and adapted from the French
by Antony Mason

For Reader's Digest
Series Editor: Christine Noble
Prepress Accounts Manager: Penny Grose

Reader's Digest General Books
Editorial Director: Cortina Butler
Art Director: Nick Clark

ISBN 0 276 42523 5

Discover the World: THE INDIAN SUBCONTINENT
was created and produced by
HUBERT DEVAUX & CO, Paris for
Selection Reader's Digest S.A., Paris, and first published
in 2001 as *Regards sur le Monde: L'INDE ET LES PAYS DE L'ASIE DU SUD*

©2001 Selection Reader's Digest, S.A.
212 boulevard Saint-Germain, 75007, Paris

CONTENTS

INTRODUCING
THE INDIAN
SUBCONTINENT

For centuries, the Indian subcontinent, with its ancient religions and dramatic landscapes, has conjured up a sense of the exotic in Western minds. This is a land of brilliant colour and ritual, redolent with intricate spices, vibrant with the strains of the sitar and tabla, thronging with humanity. Waves of invaders have cast covetous eyes upon the riches of this region, but it has consistently absorbed the impact of conquerors, and then subtly cast its spell on them. The result is a fusion of cultures that characterises India and Southern Asia today.

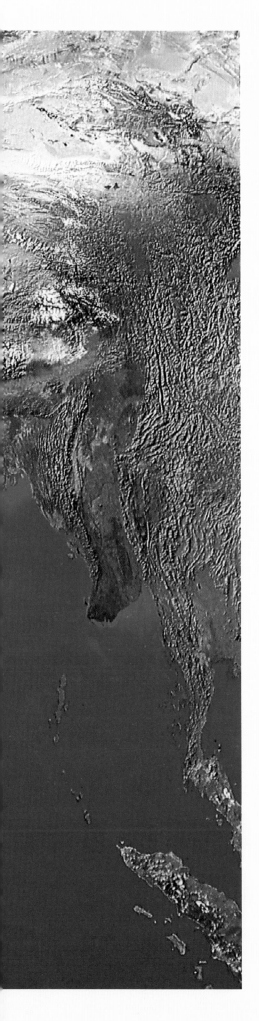

Ancient patterns

Seen from space, the Indian subcontinent looks like a vast triangle thrusting southwards into the Indian Ocean, joined to the rest of Asia by the towering Himalayas. A glance at a map of the world as it might have looked 150 million years ago explains how this part of the continent took shape. India once formed part of the ancient landmass called Gondwanaland, from which Africa, South America, Antarctica and Australia also split. India broke away from the east coast of Africa, and, trailed by Sri Lanka, headed across the ocean until it collided with Asia, forcing up the Himalayas along the line of impact. This chain of mountains now marks the northern boundary of the chunk of the Earth's crust called the Indo-Australian Plate. South-west of India is the chain of atolls forming the Maldives. They are the remnants of volcanoes that once marked the plate's western boundary, before this shifted farther west.

The rocky plateau that forms the bulk of southern India is called the Deccan. While the coastal strips and the southern tip of the peninsula are richly fertile, much of central Deccan, between the Western and Eastern Ghats, is semi-arid – although each year the heavy monsoon rains encourage the land to flourish for a brief time. North of the Deccan the landscape is dominated by the Ganges Plain, one of the world's most productive food-growing regions. Crops of rice and wheat are sustained by river water and irrigation systems. To the west, in Pakistan, the River Indus serves a similar function.

The geography and climate of Southern Asia has had a direct impact on the course of its history. Some of the oldest known cities in the world, such as Mohenjo-Daro

and Harappa, grew up on the banks of the Indus more than 4500 years ago. Later, large crop yields in the Ganges Plain permitted the growth of trade and provided the economic basis upon which culture could thrive.

The Himalayas, and their extension into the Karakoram Range, the Hindu Kush and the mountains of western Pakistan, form a barrier between India and the rest of Asia some 2000 miles (3200 km) long. Beneath this mountainous rampart, the Indian subcontinent nurtured its unique civilisation in relative seclusion. But a narrow fault in the protective barrier, the Khyber Pass, has been exploited by conquering armies as a gateway to the subcontinent since ancient times. The history of the region is thus one of repeated invasion, destruction and assimilation.

The regularity of the monsoon winds that blow across the warm Indian Ocean allowed lucrative sea-borne trade with distant lands. Ports along the coast of India became essential stopping points on the maritime trading routes that linked Europe and the Mediterranean with the China Sea. Ideas were also traded along these routes: Hinduism and Buddhism had influence well beyond the subcontinent, notably in South-east Asia and China, while Islam was spread by traders shortly after the lifetime of Muhammad. Christianity is said to have come to India with St Thomas the Apostle in AD 52.

India and Southern Asia have developed a complex mixture of beliefs, languages and lifestyles. While Buddhist monks chant ancient mantras in remote monasteries, thousands of commuters pack trains in some of the world's most densely populated cities. India has centres of computing excellence in cities where many people still travel to work by bicycle rickshaw. The subcontinent remains a region of troubled politics and religious conflict, yet India – with a population touching one billion – still manages to operate the world's largest democracy. Paradoxes and contrasts are endemic in this vast land.

The tiger's tooth and the earring The triangular shape of India has often been compared to the tooth of a tiger, while Sri Lanka hangs like a graceful pendant earring, richly coloured in its tropical lushness. The region stretches from the Equator to 35° of latitude north.

Temperamental river When it enters India in Assam, the Tibetan river called the Yarlung Zangbo becomes the River Brahmaputra ('son of Brahma'). The Assamese consider it their sacred river, with power of life and death. It serves as a means of transport and a source of fish, but when in flood it can rise 40 ft (12 m) above its normal level and spread to a width of 50 miles (80 km).

Prototype dinghy On the upper reaches of the River Indus, traditional ferries are made of inflated goat or buffalo skins. The snow melt causes powerful and unpredictable flooding, making bridge-building difficult upstream of Attock, in the north of the Punjab province of Pakistan. These precarious-looking craft have provided a means of crossing since ancient times.

Holy waters The Ganges originates high in the mountains of the Garhwal region in the heart of the Himalayas, where it takes the name Bhagirathi (far right). The source of the river is a glacier near the village of Gangotri, 25 miles (40 km) south of the Chinese border, a place of pilgrimage much visited by the sadhu holy men. According to legend, King Bhagiratha called forth the water of the Ganges in order to purify the ashes of his dead ancestors. The miracle of its creation was achieved with the intercession of Shiva.

8

Heavenly scent Large swathes of Himachal Pradesh, a mountainous state to the south of Kashmir, are covered with alpine vegetation (right). Near the trekking station Brahmaur, which stands at 6500 ft (1981 m), there are extensive forests of conifers such as the sweet-smelling Himalayan cedar or deodar (from the Sanskrit devadaru, 'wood of the gods').

Top of the world *Straddling the border between Nepal and Tibet, Mount Everest (right) rises to a majestic 29 029 ft (8848 m). The Tibetans call it Chomolungma, 'Goddess Mother of the World'.*

In the ancestors' footsteps *During the short summer months, shepherds take their flocks of sheep (left) to graze on the stony bed of the River Zanskar, near Padum, in the northern Indian state of Jammu and Kashmir. The Zanskar region remained virtually cut off from the rest of the world until recent decades and as a result it has managed to preserve a strong cultural identity. Most of its people follow a form of Buddhism that has been preserved by monks living in remote monasteries.*

Ice highway *At the northern end of the Karakoram chain in Pakistan, the Batura Wall rises to 25 540 ft (7785 m). At a height of 13 000 ft (4000 m), the Batura Glacier has carved a valley running for 35 miles (56 km). This glacier is the most accessible in the range. It is one of the highlights for trekking parties setting out from Passu, a stop on the Karakoram Highway that links Pakistan to China.*

Water world
The borderlands between the southern Indian states of Kerala and Tamil Nadu are dominated by the Nilgiri and Cardamom Hills, the southern extension of the Western Ghats. Deluged by the monsoon rains, the landscape is richly decked in forests and plantations growing coffee, tea, rubber and medicinal plants. Rivers tumble down the flanks of the hills, spilling over the rock ledges to form gushing waterfalls.

Golden city   In the far west of Rajasthan, at the heart of India's great desert, the Thar, lies the remote town of Jaisalmer, with its citadel encircled by a turreted wall of gold-hued stone. Rising from its rock plinth like a vision from the Arabian Nights, it looks out over a vast sea of sand.

Rich profusion   Granite hills create the dramatic contours of central-southern Sri Lanka (left), rising to 8281 ft (2524 m) at Mount Pidurutalagala (or Mount Pedro). Well watered by rains, particularly on the western flanks, and especially during the monsoon season, this region is covered by thick vegetation, with forests of yellow and green bamboo, ebony and mahogany, flame trees, rubber trees and areca palms, interspersed with plantations of tea, cocoa and coffee.

13

Healing powers   Near Varkala (left) in Kerala, southern India, cliffs of red sandstone line the wild beach of Papanasam, which is fringed by coconut plantations and rice paddies. Varkala, an ancient Hindu pilgrimage site sacred to the god Vishnu, is also a spa centre famed for its mineral water and mud baths.

Blue lagoon   Rihiveli, an island of silver sand (above), forms part of the south Male Atoll in the Maldives archipelago. Just 1475 ft (450 m) long and 500 ft (150 m) wide, it is surrounded by a vast lagoon of shallow water – conditions for which the local dhoni boats, with their shallow draught and rectangular sail, are ideally suited.

Fragile beauty   An aerial view of the Male Atoll shows two of the inner islands: Ihuru, just 650 ft (200 m) in diameter, and Vabbin Furu. Situated to the south-west of India, the Maldives archipelago consists of some 2000 coral islands, of which only one in ten is inhabited. The product of a volcanic fold in the Earth's crust, these atolls stand only a few feet above the sea and are under serious threat from the rise in sea levels associated with global warming.

15

A brief history

All the great civilisations of the ancient world are closely associated with rivers. The Indus and the Ganges brought fertility to the regions that they traversed, fostering ways of life, traditions and cultures that would permit the development of village economies into cities. Their success was often their undoing: the well-stocked granaries incited the greed of nomadic peoples, who descended on the towns and often remained in occupation. They brought with them successive waves of cultural change, but these consolidated over time into the Indian subcontinent's own distinctive brand of civilisation.

Spectacular remains

In 1856 railway constructors unearthed a vast stock of fired-clay bricks near the village of Harappa. Among them were seals decorated with pictographic inscriptions

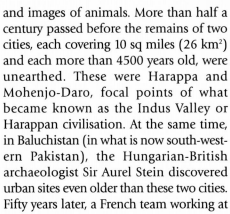

Ancient jewels Found at Mohenjo-Daro, this necklace of shaped and polished semiprecious stones (agate, rock-crystal, lapis lazuli, amber, onyx and others) dates from the 3rd millennium BC.

and images of animals. More than half a century passed before the remains of two cities, each covering 10 sq miles (26 km²) and each more than 4500 years old, were unearthed. These were Harappa and Mohenjo-Daro, focal points of what became known as the Indus Valley or Harappan civilisation. At the same time, in Baluchistan (in what is now south-western Pakistan), the Hungarian-British archaeologist Sir Aurel Stein discovered urban sites even older than these two cities. Fifty years later, a French team working at Mehrgarh unearthed the oldest vestiges of farming activities and village life, dating from the 8th millennium BC.

A further, spectacular extension of this story was announced in January 2002. Indian oceanographers, surveying the Gulf of Khambhat, off the coast of Gujarat to the south-east of the Indus delta, discovered two huge, regular, grid-like structures on the seabed, at a depth of 120 ft (36 m). Shards of pottery,

Water of life The River Indus brings fertility to the moonscape of Ladakh, high in the Himalayas.

beads and pieces of sculpted wood and bone have been recovered from the site. The carved pieces of wood have been dated to 7500 BC – 5000 years older than Harappa and Mohenjo-Daro. It appears that these cities may have been drowned by the rise in sea levels after the end of the last Ice Age, about 8000 BC. These discoveries have yet to be fully verified – but the implication is that civilisation may be far older than previously thought.

Indus civilisation

Religious ecstasy This soapstone bust from Mohenjo-Daro is thought to represent a priest-king. His tunic is decorated with trefoils, a religious symbol of the star cult.

exported cotton fabric, carved ivory and pearls. Trade was conducted by river and sea, following the coasts of the Arabian Sea and the Gulf. The Indus Valley civilisation lasted for 1000 years before coming to a sudden end in about 1700 BC. No one knows what caused its sudden demise, but nothing like it emerged until another millennium had passed. This time the new cradle of civilisation was the Ganges.

The twin cities of Harappa and Mohenjo-Daro

Lying about 375 miles (600 km) apart, Harappa and Mohenjo-Daro appear to have been the key cities of the Indus Valley. They flourished between 2500 and 1700 BC, at about the same time as other Bronze Age cultures in ancient Egypt, Mesopotamia and Crete. Built of fired brick, both cities had wide streets, complexes of public buildings, two-storey residences and workshops. Many of the houses had bathrooms connected to underground sewers. Although there were no major temples, the two cities had citadels that recall the pyramid-like ziggurats of Mesopotamia. One of the two citadels of Mohenjo-Daro has a large public pool, which suggests that ritual bathing played a role in the culture, as it still does in India today. No major grave sites have been found, but excavations have revealed sculpture and clay models, jewellery, weights and measures, and even dice made to the same pattern as modern dice. The clay seals show that they had writing, but it has not yet been properly deciphered.

Dancing girl   This cast bronze figurine from Mohenjo-Daro dates from the 3rd millennium BC.

Brickwork   In the lower city of Mohenjo-Daro (below), low walls composed of thousands of fired bricks surround a circular well.

Signed and sealed   A soapstone seal from Mohenjo-Daro shows totemic symbols of a bull's head (in mirror image) beneath a tree of life. Seals were used to authenticate clay documents, such as lists accompanying consignments of goods.

From the Indus to the Ganges

The rich alluvial soil of the Indus Valley fostered the development of grain cultivation. Vast granaries indicate crop surpluses, which provided the basis for trade with the city-states of Mesopotamia, in modern Iraq, where many seals from Harappa and Mohenjo-Daro have been found. As well as wheat, the people of the Indus Valley

Aryan divinity   Indra, the Aryan god of war, depicted on the back of an elephant.

The Aryan invasion

The earliest sacred texts of Hinduism, in particular the *Rig Veda*, have their own theory of what happened to the cities of the Indus Valley: they were invaded and destroyed by the Arya, or Aryans, a people who may have originated in the area around the Caspian Sea, or southern Russia. In about 1500 BC these fair-skinned, warlike peoples descended from the Iranian plateau and overwhelmed the Indus Valley with their bows and horse-drawn chariots. They then moved into the Punjab, the 'Land of Five Rivers' that now spans the border between India and Pakistan. This invasion may have been less dramatic than the *Rig Veda* suggests: it is more probable that small groups of nomads settled these lands, mixed with the local population and achieved a position of authority that gave them political ascendancy. Hitherto, the Land of the Five Rivers had been the territory of darker-skinned people who spoke Munda and Dravidian languages, and who now live primarily in central and southern India.

The emergence of caste

Several key cultural changes occurred under this Aryan influence. Their gods were added to the local pantheon, and their rituals and animal sacrifices were accompanied by the consumption of *soma*; researchers claim that this contained an infusion of the fly agaric mushroom, which has toxic and hallucinogenic properties. More significantly, the Aryans brought their own large body of cultural and spiritual information, which was transmitted orally. The sacred *Vedas*, for example, were not written down until the 3rd century BC.

The language that they used was Sanskrit, which became the language of knowledge and religion. In Sanskrit the word *arya* means 'of noble birth'. Aryan society was divided into three classes, all superior to the conquered and enslaved peoples, who became a class of labourers – the Sudra. Thus the organisation of Indian society into castes, or *varna*, began with the arrival of the Aryan tribes. Aryan culture was strongly patriarchal, and women were treated as property.

Into the Ganges

Harried by other tribes from the west, the Aryans progressively moved eastwards, towards the Ganges, which became known as the 'Aryan homeland', or *aryavarta*. But the transition was not easy: the Ganges Plain was thickly forested and posed a challenge to people without iron tools. They survived by herding, gathering wild plants, hunting and slash-and-burn agriculture. In about 1000 BC, iron ore was discovered in the east of the Ganges Plain. From this time on, agriculture progressed rapidly. Iron axes were used to clear the forests and ploughs were fitted with iron shares. These developments led to a renaissance of urban culture. Indrapat (Delhi), Kashi (Varanasi or Benares) and Hastinapura were among the first trading settlements to blossom into towns, although they did not take on the scale of Mohenjo-Dara and Harappa.

The spiritual labyrinth

These centuries of expansion and prosperity nurtured the development of religious ideas, from which Hinduism emerged. The concept of the transmigration of souls took hold. This proposes that the soul is reincarnated after death in a different form according to the actions of the individual during each lifetime, and the merit

Copper age   A cut-out image made from a copper sheet shows a stylised human figure. Found at Chandausi, on the Ganges Plain in Uttar Pradesh, it dates from about 1200 BC.

The Hindu golden age

Hindu tradition divides the history of the world into four ages, which form a ceaseless cycle of creation, destruction and re-creation. The first, *satya yuga*, lasts for 1 728 000 years, during which people live in truth, without pain, and with one caste. Today Hindus live in *kali yuga*, the fourth age, which will last for 432 000 years – an age of decadence leading to chaos, before the cycle begins again.

Ancient rhythms *Hand-tilling required hard physical labour. Ancient methods are still used to win crops of cotton from the arid soil of the Indus Valley in Sind province, south-east Pakistan.*

acquired. The hierarchy of the caste system was closely integrated into this belief. The Brahmans, the priestly caste, held a monopoly on spiritual knowledge and power, and were thus ranked as the highest. For this reason, the religion of this period (from about 1200 to 500 BC) is often referred to as Brahmanism. The Kshatriyas, the warrior caste, were the temporal rulers, and the Vaisyas were the traders and artisans. The servants of these three castes, the workers, were the Sudras.

Elegant simplicity *This pottery bowl was found at Hastinapura, an early urban centre on the Ganges Plain. Unglazed, but decorated with floral motifs, it dates from 800-400 BC.*

Dirty work
A blacksmith hammers a machete in a workshop that has changed little since ironworking began in India. As elsewhere in the world, the work of blacksmiths was considered impure, and so they stood outside the caste system.

Holy city *Taxila, in Pakistan, was once a regional capital and a major centre of Buddhism. The town was visited in the 7th century AD by the pilgrim Xuan Zang (or Hsuan Tsang), who, like many Chinese, came to India to study Buddhism in the land of its origins.*

The rise of Buddhism

In the 6th century BC, repeated conflicts and a growing gap between rich and poor inspired a reassessment of values which resulted in the egalitarian doctrines of Jainism and Buddhism.

Jainism was founded by Vardhamana Mahavira (599-527 BC), Buddhism by his younger contemporary Siddhartha Gautama (*c*.563-*c*.483 BC), the Buddha or 'Enlightened One'. Both sets of teaching called into question the tenets of Brahmanism. They criticised the practice of sacrifice and denounced the Brahman priests, who had enriched themselves and acquired political power.

Jainism and Buddhism first took hold in Magadha (in modern Bihar), a kingdom that held strategic power over river trade in the Ganges Valley. These two religious philosophies shared many essential features: both sought salvation through the conquest of material existence; both aimed to escape from *karma* (the cycle of reward or punishment in the next life) and achieve a state of all-knowing bliss. Of the two, Buddhism became the more widespread;

its main period of influence lasted for more than 15 centuries in India, and it spread throughout eastern Asia.

Caravan routes

By the start of the 5th century BC, Magadha had begun to dominate the 16 or so warring kingdoms into which the Ganges Plain was divided. Its rich mineral resources made it a powerful kingdom, while its fertile land yielded two or three crops a year. It was the hub of a trading empire, despatching huge caravans of ox-carts in all directions, carrying sugar cane, grain, sandalwood, bamboo, metals and cotton cloth. They also carried Buddhism with them, but in areas such as the Punjab it was resisted, particularly by peasants loyal to the cult of Krishna-Vishnu, who bred the cattle used in the ritual sacrifices conducted by Brahman priests. By the 4th century BC, Magadha's power extended across most of northern India, as far as Taxila, in the upper Indus Valley, on the borders of the Persian Empire. But now a new force intervened: the armies of the Macedonian Greek, Alexander the Great (356-323 BC).

Towards the first empire

In 331 BC Alexander the Great defeated the Persians and became master of south-west Asia. He pushed on eastwards and in 327 BC invaded India, establishing a satrapy (province) in the Punjab, and founding a colony on the Indus called Alexandria Opiana. He is said at this time to have encountered the young man whom the Greeks knew as 'Sandrocottus': this was Chandragupta Maurya, who went on to seize the throne of Magadha (reigned *c*.321-297 BC) and launch an empire of his own.

Chandragupta took advantage of the chaos that followed Alexander's early death to expand his kingdom across the Indus Valley. Alexander's successor, the Macedonian general Seleucus, attempted to regain lost ground and invaded India in 305 BC, but was decisively defeated by Chandragupta in 303 BC. By the end of his reign, Chandragupta's territory, called the Mauryan Empire, stretched right across northern India, from southern Afghanistan

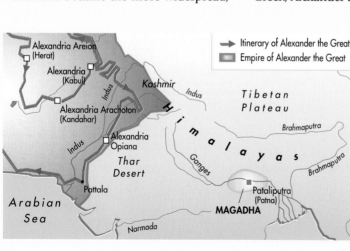

East meets West *A 15th-century miniature from the Herat school in Afghanistan depicts Alexander the Great being shown a Hindu idol during his advance into India.*

(Map legend)
→ Itinerary of Alexander the Great
▇ Empire of Alexander the Great

(Map labels) Alexandria Areion (Herat); Alexandria (Kabul); Kashmir; Indus; Tibetan Plateau; Alexandria Arachoton (Kandahar); Himalayas; Brahmaputra; Alexandria Opiana; Indus; Thar Desert; Ganges; Brahmaputra; Pattala; Pataliputra (Patna); MAGADHA; Arabian Sea; Narmada

The nirvana of Prince Gautama

According to legend, the founder of Buddhism, Siddhartha Gautama, was born in Nepal in Lumbini Park, a grove of trees sacred to the mother goddess. The son of the raja of the Sakya tribe, he enjoyed a luxurious upbringing far from the world's troubles. When he discovered the existence of suffering, illness and death, he renounced all worldly comforts. At 29 years old, he shaved his head, dressed in simple clothes and set out to discover the way to save humanity. He lived as a hermit in the jungle until one day, at Bodhgaya, seated beneath a bodhi tree, he experienced Enlightenment and nirvana (the state of deep inner freedom derived from the elimination of desire and absorption into the infinite). He spent the next 45 years spreading knowledge of this revelation: that it is possible, through meditation and practice in following the right path, to free oneself from the universal human experience of suffering. The Buddha ('the Enlightened One'), as he became known, died after achieving *parinirvana* – the state of understanding and bliss that freed him from the cycle of reincarnation.

Eternal peace   A stone relief carving dating from the 5th or 6th century AD is one of dozens of sculptures and paintings in the Ajanta caves, in central India. Here the Buddha is depicted in reclining position, achieving parinirvana (the final nirvana), moments before death.

to the Bay of Bengal, and as far south as the Narmada River. At this point, Chandragupta – so it is said – abdicated in favour of his son, became a Jain monk, and died in about 286 BC when he starved to death by fasting. His grandson Asoka completed his conquests by creating the largest empire India has ever known.

The Mauryan Empire was extraordinarily varied: primitive tribes and learned scholars able to read Aristotle's treatises in Greek could both be found within its limits. The Mauryan capital was the magnificent new city of Pataliputra (now Patna), but to ensure the efficient administration of this huge territory, Taxila and Ujjayini were proclaimed secondary capitals. Only the Dravidian far south remained outside

the Mauryan orbit, and developed it own distinctive civilisation. The Malabar and Coromandel coasts of southern India had long had trading contact with Egypt, Greece, Persia, Rome and China. In the coming centuries, the power of the Tamil kingdoms in the south would extend right across South-east Asia.

Ancient smile   The bust of a young girl, from the Maurya period (3rd-2nd century BC), was found near the Mauryan capital Pataliputra (Patna), in north-east India. Modelled in clay, then kiln-fired, it is reproduced here at approximately its real size.

The empire splinters

The reign of Asoka (c.269-232 BC), the most celebrated ruler of ancient India, brought together the virtues that have been championed by all the greatest Indian civilisations: a spirit of tolerance and assimilation, and a sense of unity. He introduced fairer laws and a welfare system, and carried out major building and engineering projects. After his death, the sheer size of his territory made the Mauryan Empire fragile; an overstretched bureaucracy and the lack of a national cohesion led to its collapse after 184 BC.

National symbol
Lions, carved in sandstone, faced all corners of Asoka's empire from the top of a high column erected at Sarnath, near Benares. This sculpture is still the emblem of the republic of India.

Asoka, the Buddhist emperor

Asoka inherited the Mauryan throne in about 269 BC. In the early years of his reign he extended his empire across the subcontinent: only the three Tamil kingdoms in the south remained outside its sphere. But Asoka became filled with remorse over the atrocities of war and the suffering of the conquered. In 250 BC he renounced war and Brahmanism and converted to Buddhism, hoping to further his conquest by *dharma* (the practice of right-living). He showed his repentance by erecting seven sculpted pillars and engraving 14 edicts in stone in all reaches of his empire. The inscriptions championed the supremacy of law above violence, and the practice of virtue and solidarity. They promoted *ahimsa*, respect for all living creatures, and the practice of non-violence. Tolerance towards other religions and sects was encouraged, but Asoka sent Buddhist missionaries far and wide. His own son, Mahinda, took Buddhism to Sri Lanka. By the time of Asoka's death in 232 BC, Buddhism had become the principal religion of the Mauryan Empire.

Pleasure dome *The rock-fortress of Sigiriya rises 650 ft (200 m) above the surrounding forests of central Sri Lanka. It was built in the 5th century AD by King Kasyapa, as a last defence against invasion by his half-brother, who had fled to India after the coup that brought Kasyapa to power.*

Hindu capital
Badami, in the central southern Indian state of Karnataka, was once the capital of the Chalukya Empire, which was ruled by a Hindu dynasty. Built at the foot of a hill of red sandstone, it was founded in the 6th century AD. Various caves and rock-cut temples are devoted to Shiva, Vishnu and Brahma, but the smallest cave is a Jain shrine, dedicated to the Mahavira, the founder of the religion.

The western provinces were attacked by invaders from Bactria and Parthia (in modern Afghanistan and Iran). First came a new wave of Greeks, then the Shaka, who settled in the lower Indus Valley and Gujarat. In the 1st and 2nd centuries AD, nomadic Kushana hordes from Afghanistan and Central Asia descended into the Indus Valley, conquered the Shakas, and forged an empire stretching from the Afghan Plateau to Magadha. Their king, Kanishka, converted to Buddhism, and

Seat of learning
The Buddhist
university at
Nalanda (in the
state of Bihar) was
founded in 427 AD.
When the Chinese
pilgrim Xuan Zang
visited it during its
heyday in the 7th
century, it had
10 000 students,
but it was destroyed
by Muslims in the
12th century.

Harsha, the poet king

Harsha Pushyabhuti (c.590-647 AD) was the son of the king of Thanesar in the Punjab, who had fought off the invading Huns. Harsha expanded his empire to cover all the Ganges Plain to the Bay of Bengal, plus part of Rajasthan, but he permitted local rulers to remain in power in return for tribute. An enlightened ruler, he was also a poet and dramatist, and was converted to Buddhism. But Hinduism was meanwhile undergoing a revival. Harsha shared his throne with his widowed sister, whom he had rescued from *sati* – the Hindu tradition by which a surviving wife threw herself on the funeral pyre of her dead husband. This fuelled opposition to his rule by the Brahmans. His assassination heralded the decline of Buddhism in India.

during his reign China opened its doors to Indian and Buddhist influence. The Kushana Empire became a meeting-point for Indian, Chinese, Central Asian and Hellenistic culture. Sanskrit was adopted as the official language of the court.

The second empire

In the fourth century AD, a new dynasty arose in Magadha, led by the Gupta family. Their first king, Chandragupta I, ascended the throne in 319 AD, and through military alliances and by marriage, expanded the kingdom to cover Bihar and parts of Bengal, thus founding the Gupta Empire. The economy burgeoned through trade with China, the Arab World and South-east Asia, and the new-found wealth funded a flourishing of religious architecture.

His successors Samudragupta and Chandragupta II expanded the empire further through conquest and marriage to cover much of the area formerly ruled by the Mauryan Empire. Chandragupta II was also noted as a liberal sovereign and a patron of the arts: his reign was one of the great cultural high points of ancient India, and the Gupta period is often called the 'Classical Era' of Indian history.

Like the Mauryan Empire before it, the Gupta Empire fell victim to new invaders. At the end of the 6th century, the Huns of central Asia conquered the Punjab and Kashmir. Once again the Ganges Plain was broken up into small warring states. It was only under the brief rule of King Harsha of Kanauj (reigned 606-647 AD) that the Ganges Plain regained any sense of unity.

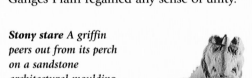

Stony stare A griffin peers out from its perch on a sandstone architectural moulding. Dating from the 1st century BC, it comes from Sanchi in Madhya Pradesh.

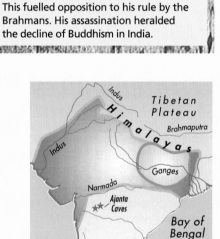

Gupta Empire ☐ under Chandragupta I
☐ under Chandragupta II

Buddhist art gallery *The richly decorated Ajanta caves served as a Buddhist monastery from the 2nd century BC to the 7th century AD. They are now preserved as a World Heritage Site.*

The Tamils: traders and warriors

While the north of the subcontinent suffered a period of political instability and religious conflict, the lands of the south, the Deccan and notably the Tamil kingdoms, enjoyed centuries of prosperity and a cultural flourish. The ports of the Coromandel and Malabar coasts had extensive trade links, allowing ideas as well as goods to travel. Jewish traders settled on the Malabar coast. Following early missionary work said to have been carried out by St Thomas the Apostle in the 1st century AD, the first Christian communities appeared. From the 7th century, Islam began to take hold in the southern Deccan, through contact with Arab merchants. Hinduism was meanwhile spreading across the subcontinent. The Tamil Pallava dynasty encouraged the construction of Hindu temples, notably those at Mahabalipuram and Kanchi (now Kanchipuram), but Buddhism and Jainism were also tolerated.

In the 9th century the Pallavas were defeated by the Cholas, also Tamil, who dominated the southern peninsula for five centuries. King Rajaraja I (reigned 984-1014) and his son Rajendra (reigned 1014-44) conquered Sri Lanka and launched military campaigns in the plains of the north. Naval expeditions set out to colonise other lands in Asia and Southeast Asia. These two kings brought thousands of Brahmans from the north to preside over the vast temples they built at Chidambaram and Tanjore.

Crowd scene   Relief sculptures at Kandariya Mahadev, the largest temple at Khajuraho, built 1025–50.

Meanwhile, in the Ganges Plain, a series of small kingdoms came and went, never able to unite long enough to create a strong state. They were called the Rajput kingdoms, after the warrior caste that dominated them, said to be descendants of the Huns and other Central Asian tribes. In the 7th century they took control of a region called Rajputana, now Rajasthan. The Chandella Rajput dynasty managed to keep hold of its throne for almost four centuries, establishing its capital at Khajuraho, famous today for the erotic sculptures that decorate its temples.

Guru Nanak, faith in one god

Guru Nanak (1469-1539), the founder of Sikhism, was born a Hindu. The son of a Lahore merchant, he worked as an accountant for the Lodhi government at Sultanpur until the age of about 30, when he had his first revelation: that all men are equal before a single god, and that Muslims and Hindus had to find a means of reconciliation. After a series of pilgrimages to the holy sites of Hinduism and to Mecca, he returned to his homeland to found a community where he preached to his disciples (*Sikh*) the virtues of tolerance, neighbourly love and belief in one god. His spiritual testament was set out later in the Sikh holy book, the *Adi Granth* or *Guru Granth Sahib*.

Arrested motion   An 11th-century bronze, from the Chola period, depicts Krishna dancing.

Former glory The remains of Vijayanagar ('City of Victory') in Karnataka, the former capital of the Hindu Vijayanagar Empire, cover 10 sq miles (26 km²). It was destroyed in 1565 by the Confederacy of the Deccan Sultans.

The first sultans of India

This lack of unity provided an opening for Muslim invaders from the north-west. Almost every year between 1000 and 1026, Mahmud, the Turkish Muslim governor of Ghazni, in Afghanistan, launched raids on the wheat granaries and temples of the Indus Valley. He was more interested in looting than in establishing rule, and used his spoils to fund military campaigns in central Asia. After his death in 1030 the Turkish threat was forgotten until the end of the 12th century, when Muhammad Ghuri (or Muhammad of Ghur) advanced across north-west India, gaining control of Delhi in 1192. His general, Qutb-ud-Din Aybak, a former slave, was put in charge of Indian affairs before being appointed Sultan of Delhi in 1206 after Muhammad Ghuri was assassinated. He was succeeded in 1210 by Sultan Iltutmish, who came under threat from the Mongol leader Genghis Khan. He abandoned the western provinces of his kingdom to reinforce his position on the Ganges Plain, but later retook the Indus Valley and annexed Bengal.

The pillage of Delhi

This first Muslim dynasty of the Delhi Sultanate was overthrown in 1290 by the Khalji dynasty, then in 1320 by the Tughluqs, under whom the Sultanate reached its greatest extent. Numerous palaces and mosques were built in Delhi during this period, but the Sultanate disintegrated rapidly as a result of internal wrangles, leaving it vulnerable to attack by the forces of the Turkic-Mongol Tamerlane in 1398. This left a trail of utter destruction: 100 000 Hindus were slaughtered in Delhi alone, and the total death toll has been put at five million. The Sultanate was in ruins and took over 50 years to recover. The new Afghan dynasty of the Lodhis (1451-1526) transferred the capital to Agra.

While some of the Deccan came under the authority of the Muslim Bahmani sultans, with whom the Hindus had struck alliances, the south of the subcontinent resisted Islam. For two centuries after its foundation in 1336, the Hindu empire of Vijayanagar kept the Muslim armies at bay, controlling a massive territory that occupied most of the south of the peninsula, with Sri Lanka serving as a tributary state.

Vasco da Gama

The Mongol invasions of central and western Asia severely disrupted the ancient silk roads, so European merchants set out to find new routes to the East. After the first voyage of the Portuguese navigator Vasco da Gama, who reached India in 1498, Portuguese merchants arrived on the west coast of the Deccan and set up trading posts to deal in spices. The Dutch, French and English soon followed.

The Sultanate of Delhi

Tibetan Plateau

Himalayas

Indus

Brahmaputra

Delhi

Indus

Ganges

Narmada

Arabian Sea

Bay of Bengal

▭ The sultanate under Iltutmish (1221–36)

Visual feast *A detail from a 16th-century casket shows a well-to-do Portuguese couple enjoying a copious meal.*

Heirs to a reconquered empire

The final wave of Asian invaders to come through the Khyber Pass were the troops of Babur the Mughal, emir of Kabul, and a direct descendant of Genghis Khan and Tamerlane. With his experienced cavalry, Babur (the name meant 'Tiger') quickly got the better of the armies of Sultan Ibrahim, the last of the Lodhi dynasty, at the Battle of Panipat in 1526, and the Rajputs at the Battle of Kanua in 1527. Despite his warlike reputation, Babur's passions were art, poetry and gardens, setting the tone for Mughal rule in northern India.

Babur died in 1530, leaving his empire to his son Humayun. He was overthrown by the Afghan leader Sher Khan in 1540, and spent a large part of his reign in exile in

Persia (modern Iran). With the help of a Persian army, he retook Delhi in 1555, but died a year later after falling from steps in his library. His throne passed to his 13-year-old son Akbar (reigned 1556-1605).

Akbar took control of his empire in 1560 and expanded it with vigour. He also centralised the administration and established a new royal capital at Fatehpur Sikri. Akbar's reign was dazzling enough to earn him the title 'the Great', and he created a heritage that permitted his successors to manage his empire for 200 years. Jahangir (reigned 1605-27) lost Kandahar, but reinforced his control over the Himalayan foothills. He shared power with his Persian wife Nur Jahan. A passionate patron of the arts, Jahangir was also a connoisseur of intoxicants, and died in a haze of opium.

Shortly after taking the throne, his son Shah Jahan (reigned 1628-58) faced trouble along his southern frontier, and ended up conquering the whole of the Deccan. He continued the work of Akbar by building mosques and palaces at Delhi, Lahore and Fatehpur Sikri. At Agra he built the splendid Taj Mahal, a mausoleum to his favourite wife Mumtaz Mahal, who died in 1631 giving birth to her fourteenth child.

The end of the Mughals

In 1657 Shah Jahan fell ill, and the following year his son, Aurangzeb (reigned 1658-1707), the last of the great Mughal emperors, seized the throne and imprisoned his father for the last eight years of

Inspiration for the Taj A pair of 17th-century Mughal miniatures, painted on ivory, depicts the Emperor Shah Jahan (1592-1666) and his favourite wife, Mumtaz Mahal.

his life. Aurangzeb expanded the empire to its greatest limits, but his hard-line Islamic policy alienated many of the groups within it, notably the Marathas, a Hindu people of western central India, whom he fought in a series of costly wars.

Military finesse This Mughal armour is more like a work of art than military hardware.

Akbar, the great mughal

Akbar was the real force behind the long-term success of the Mughal Empire. For 25 years he led military campaigns to secure control over Bengal, Kashmir, Sind, Baluchistan, Kabul and Kandahar, Rajasthan, Gujarat and the Deccan as far south as the River Godavari. He centralised his administration with a military-like civil service, and appointed a governor (*nawab*) and civil administrator (*diwan*) in each province. He built roads across his empire and introduced a uniform system of weights and measures. Like Asoka and Harsha before him, Akbar knew that he could only maintain his rule through tolerance. He made allies of the Hindus by marrying two Rajput princesses and by appointing Rajput princes to his government. He abolished discriminatory taxes levied on non-Muslims and even invited Buddhists, Hindus, Christians and Zoroastrians to debates at his court. Like his father and grandfather, Akbar actively encouraged the arts and a style of architecture, which deliberately fused Hindu and Islamic styles. The greatest miniaturists illuminated the books in his extensive library. Akbar died in 1605, from a stomach ulcer.

The Mughal Empire at the death of Akbar (1605)

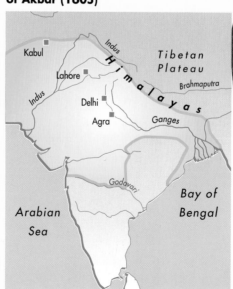

At his death, the Sikhs and Rajputs were similarly on the brink of revolt. In 1707 Aurangzeb left his tottering throne to his son Bahadur, whose brief reign was followed by a series of struggles for the succession. In 1739 the Persian Nadir Shah marched on Delhi and plundered the imperial treasure. The empire was in its death throes. For a century, the subcontinent was riven by civil wars and palace revolts – all of which were exploited by a new set of invaders, who arrived by sea.

The European conquest

After Vasco de Gama's first visit to India in 1498, European traders became regular visitors to the coasts of India. After the Portuguese came the Dutch, the French, the Danish, and the English, each seeking to secure their access to markets by establishing permanent trading posts. Backed by their armed and increasingly powerful trading companies, they fortified their ports and then began to expand outwards into neighbouring territory. The three East India Companies established by the English (in 1600), the Dutch (in 1602) and the French (in 1664) were able to exploit the disintegration of the Mughal empire by offering military services to the small kingdoms that split off from it. The colonial advance of the French and the British in the 18th century led to rivalry, from which the British emerged triumphant after Robert Clive gained Bengal in the Battle of Plassey in 1757. The Treaty of Paris of 1763, which concluded the Seven Years' War, signalled the end of French ambitions in India.

European trading posts, 17th century

Space for prayer The mosque (right) at Thatta, in Pakistan, was another of Shah Jahan's building projects, completed in 1644.

Reflected glory Camels crossing the River Yamuna (below) disturb the mirrored image of the Taj Mahal.

Defence of the realm   *A contemporary engraving depicts an Indian regiment of the British army coming under fire from sepoys during the Mutiny of 1857.*

The British Raj

In 1796 the British annexed Sri Lanka (Ceylon) and the Maldive Islands. In 1799 they took the southern Indian kingdoms; Delhi fell in 1803. The rebellious Maratha territories of the northern Deccan came under British control in 1818; Sind (the lower Indus Valley) fell in 1843, and the Punjab, the last major piece of the jigsaw, in 1849.

The British built railways, canals and roads. They introduced an effective administrative system, a postal and telegraph service, customs and a single currency. They set up schools and opened universities. They outlawed the Hindu practice of *sati* or *suttee* (the immolation of widows) and suppressed the violent crimes of the *thugee*, secret societies associated with the goddess Kali. But many Indians saw the relentless spread of Westernisation as a threat to their culture, and the increasing lack of communication between the rulers and the ruled caused a growing tide of resentment. In 1857, at Meerut, a mutiny by sepoys marked the beginning of resistance to British colonial rule.

The Indian Mutiny

The trigger for the Indian Mutiny was the delivery of Enfield rifles to the sepoys (Indian soldiers in the service of the British East India Company) in Bengal. Before loading the cartridges, the sepoys had to use their teeth to tear off the packaging, which, allegedly, had been greased with beef and pork fat.

This offence to both Muslims and Hindus was the spark that inflamed a growing sense of discontent, and in May 1857 a mutiny broke out at the barracks of Meerut. With the support of a number of maharajas and civilians, the sepoys captured Delhi and Cawnpore and laid siege to the British garrison of Lucknow. Widespread atrocities were committed by both sides before the British finally suppressed the revolt in 1859.

Hate figure   *Tipu Sultan's grisly toy, made in about 1790, shows a British officer succumbing to an attack by a tiger. His death-throes can be heard by turning the handle on the tiger's flank, which operates a small organ hidden inside.*

From resistance to independence

Queen Victoria was proclaimed Empress of India in 1876 and administering the country became the responsibility of the British crown. In 1885 the Indian National Congress was founded, which lobbied for a greater share of political power. In 1915 Gandhi set about turning the Congress Party (as it became known) into a vehicle for a popular independence movement. He organised a campaign of passive resistance against the British, using strikes, boycotts and marches. This was supported by the Muslim League, but in 1940 its leader, Muhammad Ali Jinnah, fearing an independent India dominated by a mainly-Hindu Congress Party, called for the creation of a separate Muslim state.

In 1945 the Congress Party, led by Jawaharlal Nehru, accepted the principle of two independent states. On August 15, 1947

The industrial age   *The arrival of the railway is depicted in a 19th-century mural in a merchant's house in Rajasthan.*

Two leaders *Gandhi (right) pictured with Jawaharlal Nehru in Bombay in 1946.*

The struggle for stability

The old British possessions of the subcontinent are now all independent republics: Sri Lanka won independence in 1948, the Maldives in 1965. Each country has experienced further conflict since independence. Pakistan and Bangladesh in particular have suffered frequent military coups; the Maldives had to call on the assistance of India during an attempted Tamil coup in 1988. Since 1983 Sri Lanka has been riven by civil war between the Tamil minority in the north (represented by the Tamil Tiger guerrilla force) and the Sinhalese majority, although 2002 brought some hopes for peace.

India has suffered episodes of internal unrest. In 1984 Prime Minister Indira Gandhi was assassinated by two of her Sikh bodyguards, following her suppression of a Sikh secessionist movement in the Punjab. Her son Rajiv Gandhi succeeded her, but was himself the victim of a bomb detonated by a female Tamil Tiger in 1991. India and Pakistan remain sworn enemies. Kashmir, claimed by both India and Pakistan, has been a source of contention and sporadic border fighting since Partition, and has been divided in two along the Line of Control since 1949.

independence was declared, but the Partition of the country into India and Pakistan proved complex, as Hindu and Muslim populations were mixed on both sides of the border. The movement of people descended into chaos and violence and an estimated one million died. Pakistan was divided into West and East Pakistan, separated by 1000 miles (1600 km) of Indian territory. It proved unworkable, and in 1971 East Pakistan broke free and became independent as Bangladesh.

Family tragedy *Rajiv Gandhi (with the white hat) stands before the funeral pyre of his mother Indira, in Delhi, in October 1984. Beside him are his daughter Priyanka and wife Sonia.*

Triumph *Independence for Bangladesh in 1971 was celebrated in the streets of the capital Dacca by the first president, Mujibur Rahman.*

Gandhi, the 'Great Soul'

Mohandas Karamchand Gandhi (1869-1948) was born in Gujarat and trained as a lawyer in London. He practised briefly in Bombay before going to South Africa in search of work. There he defended the rights of immigrant Indians and battled against racial discrimination. He returned to India in 1915, and preached non-violent resistance against the injustices of the British colonial regime, a policy that struck a deep chord after the massacre of Indian nationalists by British troops at Amritsar in 1919. He soon became the leading figure in the Indian National Congress. Adopting very simple dress and a modest lifestyle, he fought for recognition of the Indian identity and was a key player in the negotiations for independence. For him the process was marred by Partition, and the struggles between Hindu and Muslim communities led to his assassination by a Hindu fanatic. Gandhi was affectionately known as the Mahatma ('Great Soul'), and admired around the world for his devotion to peaceful change.

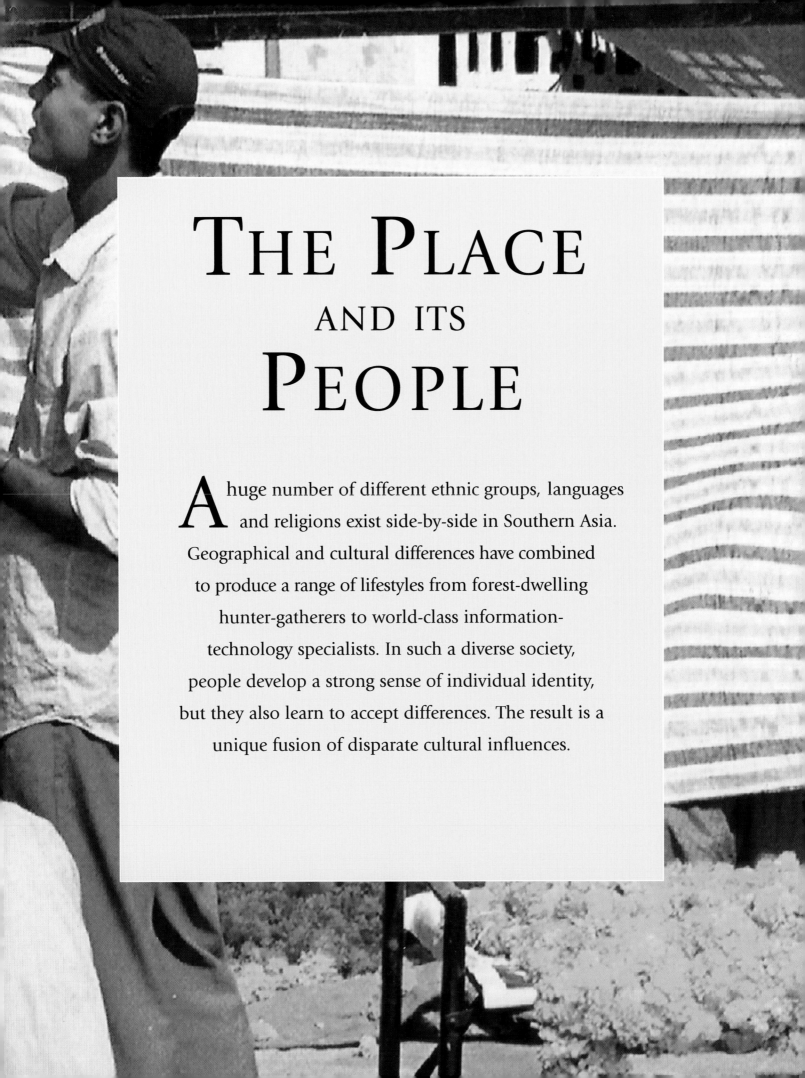

THE PLACE
AND ITS
PEOPLE

A huge number of different ethnic groups, languages and religions exist side-by-side in Southern Asia. Geographical and cultural differences have combined to produce a range of lifestyles from forest-dwelling hunter-gatherers to world-class information-technology specialists. In such a diverse society, people develop a strong sense of individual identity, but they also learn to accept differences. The result is a unique fusion of disparate cultural influences.

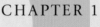

CHAPTER 1

LIVING WITH FORCES OF NATURE

The four corners of the Indian subcontinent show the region's geographical extremes. The far eastern limits are lined by the rain-soaked forests of the Chin Hills and Arakan plains on the border with Burma. In the far west, on the other hand, lie the arid hills of Baluchistan, which straddle Pakistan's border with Iran, while Rajasthan is dominated by the Thar desert, covering an area the size of Britain. The Deccan in the south is a rocky, raised plain, framed by the Ghats, which provide the backdrop to lush, tropical coasts. In the north the snow-capped peaks of the Himalaya and Karakoram ranges rise into the chill air. Weather patterns are dominated by the seasonal monsoon winds. Each June, black clouds, heavy with rain, bring relief from the stifling summer heat. The rains fall for four months, watering the rice-fields, but they can become torrential, turning the rivers into raging seas of mud.

A richly fertile valley in Swat in Pakistan, tucked away in the foothills of the Hindu Kush.

In the lands of the gods, the Sherpas and the yeti

Across the southern slopes of the Himalayas lie a string of territories so remote that for centuries they were barely known to the outside world – Ladakh, Nepal, Sikkim and Bhutan. But modern communications are bringing these countries out of seclusion, and their spectacular scenery and unique cultures attract adventurous travellers.

Demon spirit *A masked dancer at Tikse monastery, Ladakh.*

It seems natural that ancient spiritual beliefs endure in the distant lands of the Himalayas. Here on 'the roof of the world' people live in isolated valleys, surrounded by severe and beautiful peaks that are said to be the dwelling places of the Buddhist and Hindu gods. It is a landscape that resists modern influences, and inspires wonder, humility and meditation.

Next to heaven

Buddhism and Hinduism co-exist in these lands. In Nepal, the largest independent country in the Himalayas, 90 per cent of the people are Hindu. But Buddhism thrives in remote monasteries, where communities of monks pursue lives of deep meditation from early childhood, and take part in chanted rituals that have changed little for hundreds of years. They follow the Tibetan or Mahayana form of Tantric Buddhism, which, with its complex cosmology of saints (*bodhisattvas*), demons and gods,

Rhododendron *This is the national flower of Nepal.*

Window dressing *Brightly decorated houses in the Paro district of Bhutan.*

differs considerably from the Theravada Buddhism of Sri Lanka and South-east Asia. Largely suppressed by the Chinese in Tibet itself, arcane Buddhist practices, including colourful festivals with elaborate costumes and masks, persist in the remotest regions such as Mustang in northern Nepal, or Ladakh in north-western India.

Land of the Thunder Dragon

Buddhism is the main religion of Bhutan, a deeply spiritual, secretive and fiercely independent country, which limits contact with foreigners by issuing only a few thousand tourist visas every year. Also known as Druk Yul ('Land of the Thunder Dragon'), Bhutan is ruled by the 'Dragon King'. A virtually medieval

Load bearing *Sherpas head across one of the many suspended footbridges that link the remotest valleys.*

economy based on farming supports some 1300 fortress-like monasteries, or *dzongs*; the people are poor, but the regime is benign. About a quarter of Bhutan's population are Hindus of Nepalese origin, living mainly in the lowland south, and there is some ethnic tension between the two groups. In neighbouring Sikkim, sandwiched between Bhutan and Nepal, about two-thirds of the population are Hindus of Nepalese origin. The rest are mostly Buddhists, and there are several large monasteries. Sikkim was formerly a kingdom, but became a protectorate of India in 1947, and a state of India when the monarchy was abolished in 1975.

Ladakh lies high on the eastern rim of Kashmir, the region disputed by India and Pakistan. Buddhist monasteries, and a few nunneries, nestle among the rocky hills and valleys. Here, monks practise the tradition of long-term isolated meditation, walled up in a cell for three years, three months, three weeks and three days, during which they are said to come into contact with the gods.

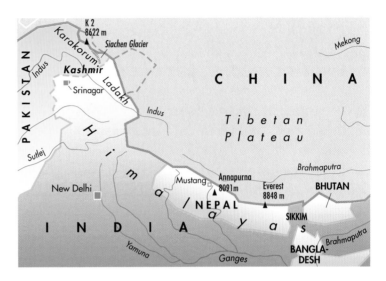

Yak country

In the higher mountain areas of the Himalayas, fertile land is found only in the river valleys and the growing season is limited. Farmers grow grain and pulses, and raise sheep, goats and yaks on the vertiginous pastures. Yaks are a variety of domesticated cattle used as a beast of burden and a source of milk, meat, hair (for fabric) and dung (for fuel). The Buddhist Dolpo-pa people of north-west Nepal still use them to carry salt across high mountain passes from Tibet, to exchange for the grain brought north on the backs of sheep and goats from the foothills of the Himalayas by Hindu herders.

Rhododendrons and the yeti

Nepal makes a virtue of its mountainous landscape by promoting tourism. Trekking and mountain climbing now provide a major source of revenue. The Sherpas of northern Nepal, a Buddhist people, have diversified from yak-herding and farming by developing their skills as mountain guides, camp attendants and porters. Expeditions set off from remote villages to begin their slow ascent, first through terraced mountainsides, then through forests of cedar, pines and spruce, which grow at an altitude of 13 000 ft (4000 m). On the lower slopes, hikers and climbers can admire a number of plants now common in the West – rhododendrons, various lilies, orchids and primulas – in their natural setting. Originally from the Himalayas, these came to Europe as the trophies of daring and devoted plant-hunters during the Victorian era.

Higher up, among the glacial lakes and plunging escarpments, live ibex, mountain goats and snow leopards, animals which are now so rare that they have acquired an almost mythical status. But the real stuff of legend is the yeti, or 'abominable snowman', which is supposedly a kind of giant ape. The *meh-teh* has long been part of Sherpa mythology, and sightings and footprints have been recorded by Western mountaineers since 1921, leading to speculation that they represent a small population of humanoid creatures; a lost branch of the human family. But the evidence remains tantalisingly elusive.

Wind and a prayer *Buddhist prayer flags flutter over a typically bare and arid mountain ridge in Ladakh. Prayers carried on the breeze are said to help deliver humanity from ignorance and suffering.*

Sacred river, polluted water

Fed by melting snows and by the torrential rains of the monsoons, the Ganges flows for 1568 miles (2525 km) from its source in the Himalayas to its sweltering delta on the Bay of Bengal. Along the way it irrigates the overcrowded plains that make up a quarter of the total land area of India. This is the most revered of India's holy rivers – and its pollution has become a national scandal.

Bathing with the gods   *In Calcutta during the October festival of Durga Puja, statues of the goddess Durga are floated on the Ganges.*

Observing a large gathering of pilgrims who had come to purify themselves in the Ganges, the American writer and humorist Mark Twain asserted that no microbe worthy of the name could possibly survive in such filthy water. The many towns and cities that have stood on this river for thousands of years have never developed effective sanitation, relying on the unshakeable Hindu belief that this is a sacred river, incapable of being anything but pure. Thus the holy Ganges is the recipient of urban sewage, industrial effluent, and the chemical-laden run-off from fields. A more notorious pollutant, however, is the bodies of the dead.

All along the river, especially at Varanasi (or Benares), funeral pyres burn day and night, and the ashes are then cast into the river to begin their purifying journey to the ocean. But each year some 3000 corpses are thrown unburnt into the river by families too poor to afford the expense of ritual cremation – as well as 10 000 animal carcasses. In the mid-1980s, the government released 28 000 meat-eating turtles into the river as part of the Ganges Action Plan to clean the water. It was hoped that the turtles would clear away the carrion, but most ended up in the cooking-pots of the fishermen who live on the riverbanks.

Dawn calm   *Sunrise heralds another day of devotion on the Ganges at Varanasi (Benares), one of the seven sacred cities of Hinduism. More than a million pilgrims come here each year.*

The Ganges

Ritual bathing

Besides helping the dead on their journey into the next life, the Ganges is said also to purify the living. Ritual bathing takes place all along the holy river, but the most impressive gathering of pilgrims takes place at Allahabad during the 42-day Kumbha Mela festival, held every 12 years when Jupiter enters the sign of Aquarius. Nearly 70 million Hindu devotees partake in this 'royal bath', immersing themselves in the sacred waters. The festival begins with four great purification baths led by a procession of sadhus, naked holy men who choose to live in a state of extreme asceticism, poverty and deprivation. Then, from the festival encampment that lines the river for 4 miles (6 km), tens of thousands of men, women and children wade in up to the waist to sprinkle the water over their head and shoulders. These ablutions coincide with the period when the elixir of life – four drops of

precious nectar that fell onto India during a battle between gods and demons, the largest of which landed at Allahabad – is said to be present in the water. By performing these purificatory rituals, the pilgrims can cleanse themselves of sins accumulated during all the long cycle of their previous lives. This opens the way to *moksha* – the possibility of freeing themselves once and for all from the cycle of reincarnations.

River of many names

The Hindus have more than a hundred epithets for the river, including *Ganga Ma* (Mother Ganges). It also has several different names on maps. From its source in a Himalayan glacier at Gangotri it is called Bhagirathi, after the legendary king who brought the river down to the Earth from her heavenly abode. It becomes the Ganges when the River Alakananda joins it. Close to the border with Bangladesh,

Water power A Hindu performs the ritual of Tarpana, offering a libation of Ganges water to his ancestors to bring them peace.

the Ganges divides into two main branches, as it splits into the world's biggest delta. One branch flows into Bangladesh as the Padma, which joins the Jamuna (Brahmaputra) to form the Meghna. But the southern branch, staying on the Indian side, is considered to be the proper continuation of the Ganges, although in its lower reaches (around Calcutta) it is known as the Hugli (or Hooghly). The Ganges is also said to flow through the heavens and through the depths of the Earth, but under names known only to the gods.

Legendary river

The Ganges was revered by the Aryans when they settled in the Ganges Plain over 3000 years ago, and they built temples all along the river for ritual bathing, sacrifice and disposal of the dead. In legend, the goddess Ganga, the personification of the river, was the daughter of Himavat, the god of the snows. She was induced to descend to Earth by the devotions of King Bhagiratha, who wanted her to purify the ashes of his 60 000 ancestors, so they could attain paradise. Ganga descended in such a torrent that only the intervention of the god Shiva, who caught the water with his matted hair, saved the earth from flooding.

Written in stone At Mahabalipuram a 7th-century relief carving recounts the story of the origins of the Ganges.

Floods and cyclones

The north of the Bay of Bengal runs into an arc of low-lying land, much of it held in the slippery clasp of the giant delta formed by the Ganges and the Brahmaputra. This region is constantly under threat of flooding, caused by torrential monsoon rains, aggravated by deforestation upstream, and rendered catastrophic by devastating typhoons.

For centuries, Bengal was known as 'Golden Bengal' because of its fabulous wealth. But during the 20th century population growth, economic stagnation and a pitiless climate led to its impoverishment. In 1947 Bengal was split down the middle to form East Pakistan (now Bangladesh) and the Indian state of West Bengal, which includes Calcutta. Bangladesh drew the short straw: a flat land, already saturated with water, it has suffered terrible floods in recent decades. Tropical cyclones sweep in from the Bay of Bengal, often accompanied by storm surges in the form of vast waves that devastate the flimsy villages of mud houses built on the low-lying islands in the delta.

Of the world's ten most deadly storms of the 20th century, seven occurred in Bangladesh. In 1970, a cyclone accompanied by a 50 ft (15 m) tidal wave surged up the delta and an estimated 300 000 people died, either in the flood, or from the diseases that spread in the aftermath. In 1988, about 28 million people were rendered destitute when the worst monsoon flooding in history affected two-thirds of Bangladesh. Another cyclone in April 1991 hit eastern Bangladesh, killing about 140 000 people.

Neighbours in need

West Bengal's neighbour to the south-east is the Indian state of Orissa, much of which consists of coastal plains, with its largest city, Cuttack, at the head of a delta formed by the River Mahanadi. In 1955 monsoon flooding submerged 10 000 villages around Cuttack and 1700 people died. In 1971, 10 000 people were killed by a cyclone. And in October 1999, the entire coastal region of Orissa was devastated by a cyclone: some 15 million people – 40 per cent of the state's population – were affected, and many thousands died. The state's main port, Paradwip, was devastated, and its main shipping lane blocked by sunken trawlers.

Life in a watery labyrinth

Constrained by poverty, the people here have little choice but to continue living under threat, eking out a living by farming the fertile alluvial soils of the delta. Hundreds of storm shelters have been built in Bangladesh in recent decades, and satellite tracking

Wetlands   Every year 60–100 in (1500–2500 mm) of rain falls on lowland Bangladesh. While awaiting more advanced flood-control systems to protect them, the people of the region keep dry by any means they can.

Borderline survival   A boatman in the Sundarbans stops for a lunch break. The region's nature reserve, classed as a World Heritage Site by UNESCO, straddles the border between India and Bangladesh.

The threat of water *Catastrophic flooding hit Bangladesh again in 1998. The regular occurrence of natural disasters is a major obstacle to development, and more than 50 per cent of the population live below the poverty line.*

has permitted the authorities to organise evacuation. In 1997, a cyclone hit Bangladesh but more than 500 000 people had been evacuated from the most exposed region and the eventual death toll of 67 could have been much higher. However, the only way to protect the region properly would be an efficient system of irrigation and dykes, requiring complex engineering and a huge financial commitment beyond the reach of Bangladesh and India.

The Sundarbans

The very heart of the Ganges delta is less prone to natural disasters because it is relatively under-populated and remains barely developed. All along the coastal borderlands between India and Bangladesh stretches an aquatic world of mangrove swamps and

rain forest called the Sundarbans. Inland, the canalised rivers, called *bihls*, criss-cross the countryside. The scarce fragments of usable land are colonised by fishermen and farmers, but their villages are under constant threat of flooding. The fishermen move about in this labyrinth of land and water on craft made of bamboo, setting up their nets to catch fish on the rise and fall of the tide.

Some 1000 sq miles (2590 km²) of the coastal tidal marshlands and mangrove swamps have been designated a nature reserve, the home of chital deer, wild boar, monkeys, countless bird species and about 250 Bengal tigers.

Aftermath *The people of Orissa found refuge among the fallen trees after the typhoon of 1999, during which winds reached speeds of more than 185 mph (300 km/h) and tossed up waves 50 ft (15 m) high. Some 5 million dwellings were destroyed, leaving millions of people homeless.*

The Thar Desert

A desert the size of Britain stretches across the borderlands of north-western India and southern Pakistan. Various semi-nomadic peoples live here in defiance of the inhospitable conditions. The men wear bright turbans coloured with vivid natural dyes, while the women glitter with silver jewellery.

Eating on the move *Camel herders prepare their evening meal.*

The Thar or Marusthali Desert, also known as the Great Indian Desert, is the most easterly of the band of tropical deserts that stretches around much of the globe along the line of the Sahara. It is shared by India and Pakistan, and their border cuts through the region. This desert has always served as a crossroads, providing vital trade links between the fertile lands of the Indus and the Ganges, and between the lands of the Deccan and the Khyber Pass. Only those with a knowledge of the land gleaned over centuries could travel through this unforgiving waste of ochre sands, where in May and June temperatures may reach 120°F (49°C). Along these trade routes came huge caravans of camels, bearing silks from China, spices from South-east Asia, silverware, hand-woven carpets, gems and opium. They stopped at the few cities along the way, such as Jaisalmer, Bikaner and Jodhpur – cities that became rich with trade, and were jealously protected by the fortresses of their rulers.

Nomads and settlers

The Thar is the world's most populated desert, due to traditions of nomadic herding, dryland farming and the extension of irrigation schemes. Adaptability has long been a crucial skill in a region barely touched by the monsoon rains. Although the desert can receive up to 20 in (510 mm) of rain a year, whole years can pass with no rain at all.

The Pushkar fair

At the full moon in the month of Kartik (October-November), a major religious festival is celebrated at the village of Pushkar in Rajasthan. The town is built around a huge scoop of ground, which, according to legend, was created by a lotus flower dropped from the hand of the god Brahma. Hindu pilgrims gather to purify themselves in the lake water. This is also the time of the Pushkar Fair, where cattle, camels, goats and sheep are sold. The festival draws sadhus, storytellers, camel racers, dancers and showmen with chained bears.

The Rabari of Rajasthan and Gujarat are one of the semi-nomadic peoples who live in the less arid margins surrounding the desert. If it rains sufficiently during the year, millet – a crop that requires little water – is planted around their villages of circular, thatched houses. In harder years, they move on with their flocks of camels, sheep and goats, seeking the pastures that spring up in the desert after sporadic rains. The Rabari men present a proud image, in their tailored and embroidered clothes and brightly coloured turbans made of long strands of cloth. The women wear long, skirts or dresses with trailing shawls, and are heavily adorned with silver jewellery, effectively carrying their family wealth around their necks, on their arms and ankles, and in their ears and noses.

Set apart The distinctive dress of the Rabari herdsmen symbolises their singular way of life. Rabari roughly means 'outside the way'.

The precious waters of the Rajasthan canal

For over a century, a growing population has placed ever greater pressure on the land, resulting in over-grazing and a cycle of land-degradation. To counteract this trend the Bhakra Dam and the Nangal Barrage were built in the 1950s and 1960s on the River Sutlej, as it exits the Himalayas, to supply water to the Rajasthan Canal (or Indira Gandhi Canal). Running for 426 miles (692 km), and with 4346 miles (6993 km) of tributaries, this irrigation system brings precious water to the northern areas of the desert, making settled agriculture possible. Farmers produce crops such as millet, sorghum, maize, wheat, barley, pulses, oil seeds, cotton and tobacco.

In Pakistan an older irrigation system in the Himalayan foothills has likewise helped to control the water supply at the edges of the Thar Desert, but much of the land irrigated by these canals has been poisoned by salinity – the build-up of the mineral salts left behind as water evaporates rapidly in the searing sun.

Camel showroom The day begins at the Pushkar Fair. Each year the fair attracts 200 000 visitors – buyers, breeders, pilgrims and tourists.

The metropolis of the Thar

A fortress town built on a plinth of yellow sandstone, Jaisalmer was founded in the 12th century on the route linking India to the Khyber Pass. The upper town is an architectural masterpiece, lying within the protection of thick walls and 99 semicircular bastions. The antiquity and opulence of the Jain temples, built in the 12th to 15th centuries, bear witness to the great fortunes amassed from trade and caravan traffic. The town's wealthy merchants built beautiful mansions called *havelis*, richly decorated with carved sandstone. Many now show signs of the neglect that has come with declining trade, and today Jaisalmer bustles with passing tourists rather than merchants.

41

The Malabar Coast: a history rooted in the spice trade

Separated from the rest of the subcontinent by the Western Ghats, the Malabar Coast of Kerala and Karnataka has followed its own course through much of history, influenced by its contact with the world beyond its seas. Sailing ships from both the Far East and the West arrived on the monsoon winds, in search of precious spices.

The Malabar Coast is one of the world's most important spice-growing regions: spices such as cardamom, ginger and pepper grow well in the humid climate. For many centuries, the ports had trade links that stretched eastwards as far as the Moluccas in Indonesia – the fabled 'Spice Islands', where cloves and nutmegs grew. In ancient times, Phoenician and Greek sailors made their way down the coast. Christians and Jews settled here early in the last millennium, many centuries before the Portuguese navigator Vasco da Gama opened up the 'Pepper Route' to European traders.

The 'backwaters'

The unusual geography of this region is the product of the copious rainfall it receives. Much of the coastal plain is pierced by a patchwork of 29 large, palm-fringed lakes, linked by rivers and canals. This web of waterways, known as the 'backwaters', surrounds islands where there are clusters of houses that stand on stilts. Their inhabitants raise cattle and chickens and have small vegetable gardens, while the plantations close by grow the cash crops that form the basis of Kerala's economy: rice, copra and coconuts, cardamom, tea, cocoa, coffee, pepper, lemons. Each is harvested in its own season, packed into cartons and then transported down the canals in long convoys of barges that zig-zag between the islands.

Along the waterways, and even in the main cities, fishermen use square, cantilevered dipping nets, a technique said to have been imported by Chinese merchants and sailors from the days of Emperor Kublai Khan in the 13th century. But for several decades now, the region has suffered from more efficient fishing methods introduced by the Norwegians. In 1954 a cooperative venture between India and Norway led to India's acquisition of a fleet of trawlers. In the 1980s nearly 2500 of these boats, designed for deep-sea fishing, worked off the coast of Kerala, raking the seabed, the coastal ecosystem, and dramatically reducing fish stocks.

Thoroughfares Barges, often loaded with rice, ply the canals and lagoons of the backwaters.

Kerala, sharing the benefits

In 1956 the principalities of Travancore and Cochin, and the Malabar district of Madras state, united to form Kerala. A year after unification, Kerala became the first state to elect a communist government. Since then, complex political alliances have reflected its diverse ethnic and religious composition, but the effect seems to be broadly beneficial. The most heavily populated state in India, but by no means the richest, Kerala's wealth is comparatively evenly distributed among its people, the Malayalis. It has the lowest infant mortality rate and the highest literacy rate in all India.

Vertical lift The fishermen of Kerala use Chinese-style dip nets on wooden frames and spars.

Sri Lanka, emerald island

Marco Polo called the island known then as Ceylon 'the most beautiful island, and the most coveted'. After two decades of independence from Britain, it took the name Sri Lanka, meaning 'blessed island'. But civil war has blighted its prosperity.

Handpicked   *Only very tender tea leaves and buds are picked.*

Sri Lanka is no bigger than Ireland or Tasmania: few places on Earth offer such a range of natural splendours in such a small space. The dry northern plains of the Jaffna peninsula contrast dramatically with the dense vegetation of the Rajarata rainforest in the centre of the island – where there have been two royal capitals – and with the lush, cool and spectacularly beautiful hill country to the south. Quite different again are the humid coasts of the south-east, where the beaches are lined with slender coconut palms leaning out over the waves.

An emerald in the Indian Ocean

Sri Lanka is often compared to an emerald lying upon the blue jewel case of the Indian Ocean. It is separated from southern India by the Palk Strait, which has at its narrowest point a channel called Adam's Bridge; a 20 mile (32 km) stretch between Rameswaram and Mannar, dotted with reefs and sandbanks. This was crossed on foot by the first inhabitants, who came from India during the last Ice Age, before the island was finally separated from the mainland by rising sea levels.

In the hills around Nuwara Eliya, in the centre of the island, tea plantations stretch as far as the eye can see, clustering around the big English-style houses of the plantation owners. Tea replaced coffee as the main plantation crop after the 1870s, when a leaf disease demolished the coffee plantations. Sri Lanka is now the world's third largest tea producer, with a crop of 295 000 tons in 2001.

At independence, Sri Lanka enjoyed one of the highest standards of living in Asia. But one major problem has prevented it achieving its promise: the bitter divide between the mainly-Hindu Tamil minority in the north and the mainly-Buddhist Sinhalese in the south, which has mired the country in civil war since 1983.

Baby bath   *Young elephants receive special attention at Pinnewala Elephant Orphanage, near Kegalla.*

Ancient irrigation

Anuradhapura (capital from the 4th century BC to the 10th century) and Polonnaruwa (capital from the 11th to 13th century) are both located in the dry central-north and eastern part of Sri Lanka. From the 4th century, reservoirs or 'tanks' were built to store rainwater collected during the monsoon. Bassawak Kulama, the oldest tank near Anuradhapura, is still in use. It has a surface area of 250 acres (101 ha). Earthwork dykes, built with the help of elephants, retained the water, and canals distributed it to the fields. In the 12th century there were 620 miles (1000 km) of canals in the region. Following invasions from southern India, the cities were abandoned to the jungle and the irrigated zones became malaria-infested swamps. Since independence, many of the old irrigation systems have been renovated and integrated with new ones.

Stilt fishing   *Villagers on the south-western coast fish from poles driven into the seabed.*

43

The hidden beauties of Hunza and Ladakh

Set among valleys of stark beauty, remote farming villages in Hunza and Ladakh follow a traditional way of life, protected from the pressures of modern civilisation by the mighty barriers of the Himalayas. Among the benefits is a mysterious longevity enjoyed by some communities.

Next to god *A whitewashed stupa serves as a reminder that Tibetan Buddhism has survived intact in the remote mountains of Ladakh.*

In the far north of the Indian subcontinent, in the western reaches of the Himalayas, lies the disputed paradise of Kashmir. It is claimed, and divided virtually in two, by both India and Pakistan, while China controls the extreme north-east, also claimed by India.

Living long in Hunza

The temperamental River Hunza flows through the far west of Pakistani Kashmir, carving out a valley of celebrated beauty. The 35 000 people, mainly Ismaili Muslims, living in the valley are famous for their longevity: many people remain fit and healthy well into their 90s. They rarely suffer illnesses such as cancer and tuberculosis, and show few signs of senility in old age. They observe strict rules of hygiene regarding water storage, which is unusual for the region. Their diet, much studied by researchers, includes plenty of fruit, particularly apricots (fresh in summer, dried in winter), yoghurt enriched with germinated wheat, and very little meat.

Arid lands *The rivers that snake through Ladakh bring life to the dry landscape, which sees little precipitation apart from the winter snows and summer rains.*

Ladakh: 'Little Tibet'

People also live to a ripe old age in Ladakh. This region falls mainly in the Indian state of Kashmir, although it also spreads beyond the Line of Control (the disputed border) into Pakistan. Culturally and geographically, however, it is more akin to Tibet. Its capital, Leh, is connected to Srinagar, the capital of Indian Kashmir, by a vertiginous road, one of the highest in the world, reaching 13 432 ft (4094 m) in places, and impassable after the first snows of winter.

As in Tibet, the climate is that of a high altitude desert. At Leh, 11 529 ft (3514 m) above sea level, just 3.25 in (83 mm) of precipitation falls each year. Winters are severe, but summers are warm. In the short growing season it is possible to harvest wheat, rye and barley.

Buddhism remains the dominant religion of Ladakh, as shown by the presence of a number of monasteries. The landscape is also dotted with bell-shaped shrines, called *chorten*, or stupas. These monuments are places of homage, commemorating the life and death of a venerated saint, or enclosing sacred relics or texts. Buddhists circle around them, always to the right, chanting sacred mantras.

One woman, many husbands

Polyandry used to be a widespread practice in Ladakh: a woman could have several husbands by marrying a man and his younger brothers. This simplified issues of land inheritance, as property did not have to be divided among many sons. It also kept the population steady in a land barely able to sustain its inhabitants. Polyandry is now rare in Ladakh, although it is found among the older generation, but it is still practised in parts of neighbouring, even more remote, Zanskar Valley.

Festive dress *Every monastery in Ladakh has its annual festival, attended by citizens in their finery.*

The Maldives, a threatened paradise

The Maldives, a scattering of tiny coral atolls and reefs in the Indian Ocean, are a get-away-from-it-all paradise for affluent tourists. But they are in danger: rising sea levels threaten to overwhelm these tiny flat lands, while their coral reefs – precious sanctuaries for an astonishing range of sea life – are suffering from the shock of climate change.

The Maldive archipelago stretches 500 miles (820 km) from north to south and 80 miles (130 km) from east to west. It includes 26 atolls and several thousand islands and islets, of which about 220 are inhabited. But their total surface area amounts to just 115 sq miles (298 km²). Distance, therefore, is a key element of life in the Maldives; so, too, are the flat-bottomed boats designed to skim across the shallow waters of the lagoons.

Coral death

During the Earth Summit held at Rio de Janeiro in 1992, the president of the Maldives, Maumoon Abdul Gayoom, became the champion of the island states by drawing the world's attention to the danger posed by global warming and the rising sea levels associated with it. The islands are no more than 8 ft (2.4 m) high; water levels have risen

Essential diversity *Brightly coloured surgeonfish and angelfish dart about the coral in the shallows off the coasts of the Maldives, playing their role in highly complex webs of ecological interdependence.*

6 in (15 cm) in the past ten years. Protective measures have already been initiated: on the small islands that are particularly vulnerable to tide and wind, the inhabitants protect the beaches with coral dykes. However, the seamounts that form the geological foundations of the islands produce new islets every year, so less pessimistic observers point to the continuous cycle of building and destruction that occurs naturally in such coral-based environments.

But the coral itself has suffered in recent years, notably as a result of the rise in temperatures linked to El Niño in 1998. The delicate living organisms that build the coral reefs need constant temperatures and will suffer 'bleaching' and coral death if the sea becomes warmer. If similar climatic conditions occur again, or if global warming changes the sea markedly, the reefs will be badly affected, along with all the abundant sealife that goes with them.

Island idyll *Many of the Maldive Islands consist of little more than sand banks formed by coral on the crests of seamounts. When coconut palms and other salt-tolerant plants colonise the land, they help to secure and enrich the soil. They also provide the shade that makes these islands idyllic holiday destinations. Tourist development is carefully regulated by the government, which has forbidden any foreign ownership of the islands.*

National parks in the land of the tiger

From the Bengal tiger to the Asian elephant, from the Great Indian rhinoceros to the black panther in the rain forests of Assam, the subcontinent possesses some of the most majestic animal species in the world. For several decades India's national parks and wildlife sanctuaries have made strident efforts to preserve this exceptionally rich heritage.

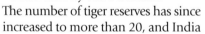

Grandstand view   *Visitors to the Kaziranga National Park in Assam can observe wildlife from the back of an elephant.*

The first national park in India was created near Dehra Dun, in the foothills of the Himalayas, in 1935. Although small at first, it was enlarged by Jim Corbett, an adventurer who was passionate about animals and after whom the park is now named. Six hours' drive from Delhi, it is home to 350 species of birds and a burgeoning population of large mammals, such as tigers, elephants and deer. There are now more than 450 national parks and wildlife sanctuaries in India, many of which started out as the old hunting reserves of the maharajas.

Tigers under threat

In 1900 there were an estimated 40 000 Indian or Bengal tigers in the Indian subcontinent: three-quarters of a century later, the number had fallen to fewer than 2000. During this time, the forests had shrunk from 40 per cent of India's land area to 15 per cent. The more aggressive predators – tigers, snow leopards, panthers – were decimated by the loss of habitat, forced to give way to the expanding human population. They were also killed, partly because they were considered dangerous, but often to satisfy big-game hunters.

In 1973 the government of Indira Gandhi joined with the Worldwide Fund for Nature (WWF) to launch Operation Tiger, setting aside nine national parks as tiger reserves. Protected breeding grounds were surrounded by buffer zones in which human activity was restricted. The number of tiger reserves has since increased to more than 20, and India has become the greatest refuge for wild tigers in the world, sheltering about half of the world's population of some 6000.

But the Bengal tiger is once more under threat. Poaching has become a greater problem than ever and accounted for the loss of

Crowned   *The sambar has distinctive three-tined antlers.*

Ruminating   *Gaurs, large wild cattle, are found in the Nargarahole National Park in Karnataka, one of the most diverse reserves in India.*

poaching than their African cousins as only the males have tusks. There are perhaps 20 000 Indian elephants left in the wild – but there were 200 000 in 1900. Forming troops of 50 or so individuals, they remain largely within the confines of reserves.

Varieties of deer, including the sambar, the axis deer or chital, and the rare swamp deer or barasingha, roam in most of the national parks. The spiral-horned blackbuck antelope was once common in northern India, but now the largest herd is in the Velavadar National Park in Gujarat. The Nilgiri tahr, a wild goat, is preserved in Eravikulam National Park, in the Western Ghats of Kerala.

There are wild as well as domestic cattle: water buffalo are found on river banks and around lakes, while the Indian bison, or gaur, lives mainly in reserves.

Temporary guest   Grebes come to nest at the Vedantangal Bird Sanctuary in Tamil Nadu.

some 300 tigers in the 1990s. During a crackdown in 2000, the police seized 350 tiger and leopard skins, and 440 lb (200 kg) of bones, claws and teeth. Much prized in Chinese traditional medicine, tiger parts are the basis of an illegal but lucrative export trade. The bones, ground into powder, are incorporated in potions used as aphrodisiacs or to promote longevity. Underfunded and understaffed, many of the parks cannot mount the surveillance and security needed to ward off poachers, who are backed by powerful trafficking organisations, and to which corrupt authorities turn a blind eye.

Seeking refuge   The golden langur, a leaf-eating monkey, is one of many rare species in Assam.

In addition, villagers, exasperated by tiger attacks on their livestock and occasionally on humans, take the law into their own hands. Those in charge of Operation Tiger now claim that unless the Delhi government takes strong action soon, the only tigers seen in India will be those depicted in advertisements.

Elephants and rhinoceroses
Smaller than their African cousins, Indian or Asian elephants are rarely more than 10 ft (3 m) high. In the wild, they live in the rain-soaked bamboo forests of Bengal, Assam, Bhutan, southern India, and in the boggy Tarai flatlands of south-eastern Nepal, where they sometimes share their territory with the Great Indian rhinoceros. Asian elephants are less vulnerable to

Birdlife   The Keoladeo National Park, at Bharatpur, Rajasthan, has 350 species of birds.

Safe haven   Some 30 tigers live in the Ranthambhore National Park in Rajasthan, a reserve covering more than 500 sq miles (1300 km²).

47

CHAPTER 2

PEOPLE AND RESOURCES

The Indian subcontinent is home to a rapidly expanding population that has put an immense strain on the land and its resources – but the outcome is not the disaster that was feared. The 'Green Revolution' in the 1960s introduced new seed strains and farming methods, and the soil has produced abundant crops. No longer struggling to feed mouths, the countries of Southern Asia have begun to produce other commodities, such as tea, coffee, sugar, rubber, cotton, jute, oil seeds, spices and cashew nuts. Industries churn out textiles, clothes, electronic goods, chemicals, coal, metals and gemstones. India has also developed its technological talents: the worldwide information revolution owes a part of its success to work done in the subcontinent. But, despite these advances, many of the cruellest aspects of under-development persist.

Planting out rice seedlings in a paddy in the state of Bihar, northern India.

India, land of rice and wheat

The population of the Indian subcontinent has tripled in half a century. During this same period, production of cereals and other arable crops has quadrupled. India now produces surpluses of both wheat and rice. But although major famines are a thing of the past, Southern Asia remains vulnerable to natural disasters and the caprices of the monsoon, which can wipe out entire crops.

High yield *Threshing in the Karakoram mountains of Pakistan.*

Every Indian eats on average 180 lb (82 kg) of rice in a year. Rice is the staple of the nation's diet, but wheat, eaten in the form of flatbreads, is a major element in Northern India.

India now ranks as the second largest rice producer in the world (after China); Bangladesh is fourth. India is also the second largest wheat producer (again, after China); Pakistan is eighth. India's wheat production (71 million tonnes) corresponds to its domestic consumption (70 million tonnes). But the annual production of rice (134 million tonnes) far exceeds its domestic consumption (82 million tonnes) and much of it is exported.

The 'Green Revolution' and self-sufficiency

Learning to cope with the conditions that led to regular famine has been a great breakthrough for India's farmers. The construction of irrigation systems during the British colonial era was the first step in the battle against drought. Then came the 'Green Revolution' in the 1960s, enabling the subcontinent to achieve self-sufficiency in cereal crop production by using new high-yield crops, fertilisers and low-tech systems of irrigation such as installing simple pumps in the wells of agricultural production areas. In regions where the conditions are most favourable, notably in the south of India, farmers produce three crops of rice in a year.

Most farms in the subcontinent are small, and many farmers do not own any land at all, but rent it from landlords, often in return for a share of the crop produced. Work in the fields follows traditional methods: ploughing with oxen, manual hoeing, harvesting with scythes, threshing and winnowing by hand. Some 60 per cent of the workforce is employed in agriculture and it remains a precarious business: in 2000, for example, drought affecting Rajasthan and Gujarat threatened two-fifths of the country with famine.

Agriculture in India

[Map showing: CHINA, New Delhi, Ganges, Indus, Calcutta, Mumbai (Bombay), Bay of Bengal, Arabian Sea. Legend: wheat, rice, millet/others]

Wheat or rice?

Southern and eastern India are rice-eating areas, while the north is mainly wheat-eating. Many people eat both: boiled rice is eaten alongside flatbreads such as chapatis, pooris and parathas. But in times of shortage people may be asked to specify their preference, and a large 'W' or 'R' will be printed on their ration cards.

Women's work *Harvesting rice in Rajasthan: women do much of the work on farms in Southern Asia.*

50

From animal sacrifice to sacred cow

In India cattle are treated with great respect, as providers of both nutrition and haulage. Their sacred status can be traced back to ancient religious texts and the time when cattle played a central role in ritual sacrifice.

Recycled energy *In regions where wood is scarce, cow dung is mixed with straw to make an efficient fuel. The dung is shaped into slabs by hand, and is then stuck to a wall to dry in the sun, as seen here in Calcutta.*

During the time when millions of cattle were being slaughtered in Europe to combat BSE ('mad cow disease'), an Indian politician proposed saving the victims by bringing them to India. The idea may have seemed far-fetched to Europeans, but not to Hindus in India, Nepal or Sri Lanka, where cattle are considered sacred and allowed to roam as they please, despite the fact that they disrupt traffic, eat crops and spread disease.

The cow is everything

In the sacred text of the *Atharvaveda* ('knowledge of magic formulas') it is written: 'He who has given a cow to the Brahmans will gain possession of all the worlds. For in the cow resides the divine Order, Holiness and Ardour. It is the Cow that brings life to the Gods; the Cow that brings life to human beings. The Cow, it is everything, everything under the Sun.' Brahman priests sacrificed the finest cows to the gods and ate beef as part of these rituals. Bones found in a number of archaeological sites provide evidence of this.

As the population increased in the Ganges Plain, more and more pasture was taken over as arable land and the consumption of beef became restricted to the high-caste elite. Then with the rise of Buddhism and Jainism, both of which criticised the practice of animal sacrifice, eating beef became taboo. The lowest ranks of society found it easy to conform to this injunction, as they were too poor to eat meat. Gradually Hinduism adopted the same attitude. Now, in a complete role reversal, Brahmans and the most devout Hindus tend to be vegetarian, while the lowest ranks within Hindu society take a more relaxed

Priority *Traffic weaves around cows in a street in Varanasi (Benares).*

view about including meat products in their diet. But not beef: cattle are protected from slaughter across India. According to Hindu tradition, the penalty for killing a cow (which is held in even greater esteem than a bull) is to suffer in hell 'for as many years as there are hairs on its body'.

Milk, butter and fuel

Despite their status, most cattle have to work to earn their keep. Since ancient times, farmers have used cattle for ploughing and for drawing a cart. They also kept one or two cows for breeding and to provide milk to make yoghurt and clarified butter (ghee), a key ingredient in Indian cooking. These days most of the milk and milk products consumed by city dwellers are produced by semi-industrial cooperatives. India has nearly 200 million head of cattle, the largest cattle population in the world, and is the second biggest producer of milk and butter.

Party dress *Cattle during the Hindu festival of Holi, when coloured powder and water are thrown around.*

Cotton, silk and cashmere

For 2000 years the Silk Roads crossed Asia, linking India and China with the Middle East and Europe. But the trading caravans carried other textiles as delicate and as prized as silk, such as the finest cotton and woollen cloth.

For the Romans, silk and cotton textiles ranked among the greatest luxuries, but China and India were their only source of the raw materials. How and where cotton cultivation began is still a mystery. It was once thought that the Indus Valley was the original source, but the discovery of cotton fibres in Mexico dating from 5800 BC has shown that cotton-weaving developed wherever the 'wool tree' grew naturally.

As good as wool

Herodotus, writing in the 5th century BC, mentioned the fruits of an Indian bush that produced wool as fine as that of sheep. In the 2nd century AD the Greek writer Arrian gave this description: 'The Indians wear linen clothes [having never seen the plant, Arrian confuses the two textiles]. They harvest this linen from trees. Indian linen has a whiteness that is far more dazzling than that of any cloth, unless it be the dark skin of those that wear it that makes it appear thus.' It was only after the Muslim conquests that cotton cultivation came to the Mediterranean. The Arabs called the plant *qutn*, the origin of the word cotton.

Southern Asia remained the main producer of cotton. When they colonised the region, the East India Company developed cotton plantations and raw cotton was shipped to British textile manufacturers.

Today, India and Pakistan rank among the top four cotton producers in the world (after China and the USA). Following improvements in fibre production during the 'Green Revolution' in the 1960s, investment in textiles has increased and in just 20 years cotton production in both countries doubled. In India, 16 out of the 21 states grow cotton, notably Gujarat and Maharashtra; in Pakistan the provinces of Punjab and Sind are leading producers.

Colour sense Textile manufacturers in Rajasthan now use synthetic aniline dyes instead of vegetable dyes.

The finest wools

The famous Kashmir mountain goats, the source of cashmere wool (also called *pashm* or pashmina), in fact come from Ladakh and the western part of Tibet. Raised by nomads at a height of over 13 000 ft (4000 m), they are protected from the cold by their thick wool. The underfur is exceptionally soft, but it is also expensive as it takes a goat four years to produce enough wool for a cashmere or pashmina shawl. In the 19th century the fashion for cashmere shawls brought work to hundreds in and around Srinagar, the capital of Kashmir, whose Maharaja had a monopoly on the supply of Tibetan wool. Craft-based production continues in the high valleys of the Himalayas and Karakorum chain, and in the Kathmandu Valley of Nepal. Meanwhile, the silk workshops of Varanasi (Benares) or Kanchipuram in Tamil Nadu are still famed for their hand-woven silk cloth.

Raw material Piles of raw cotton await processing in Gujarat, India's leading cotton-growing state.

Tea: a very British legacy

Darjeeling, Assam, Ceylon – the names of many of the most famous teas suggest that they are of South Asian origin. Far from it: as in Europe, tea-drinking is a comparatively recent habit, imported by the British, who brought bushes from China so they could produce tea for export. The people of Southern Asia have made it their own, adapting the drink to suit local tastes.

The cup that cheers *In Rajasthan, as in most of India, tea is usually served in glasses, sweetened with sugar and mixed with milk.*

In Kashmir, tea is perfumed with cardamom; on the Coromandel Coast of Tamil Nadu and Andhra Pradesh, it is spiced with pepper, cloves and chilli, and mixed with milk. In Ladakh, it is mixed with fermented yak butter to form a rich, soupy drink – an acquired taste viewed by uninitiated Western travellers as something of a challenge.

The tea kings

Tea came to India when the East India Company grew tired of its dependence on the whims of the Chinese authorities who, in an effort to curb Western expansionism, had imposed heavy taxes on tea. With European and American demand increasing rapidly, the British decided to plant tea wherever possible in their colonies. Tea made the fortune of a number of businesses, such as Twinings, founded as a tea company in 1706. In 1837 Queen Victoria granted Richard Twining II the first royal warrant for tea.

In 1894 Thomas Lipton, who began as a grocer in Glasgow, bought up coffee plantations in Ceylon that had been decimated by disease and planted them with tea. Trading under such slogans as 'Direct from the tea to the teapot' and 'If you want the best tea go to the firm that grows it', he became a millionaire and was knighted by Queen Victoria.

These days, India plays a much greater role in the tea trade. In 2000 the famous British company Tetley Tea, founded in 1856, was bought by Tata Tea Limited, which is part of the powerful Indian Tata conglomerate. Tata Tea now owns more than 20 per cent of India's various branded teas. This represents a major slice of the market in the world's greatest tea-drinking nation, which consumes 655 000 tonnes of tea each year.

Fresh tea *Sri Lanka depends on the nimble fingers of its pickers to maintain its position as the world's third largest producer of tea, after India and China.*

The flavours of the soil

The tea bush is in fact a tree, *Camellia sinensis*. It flourishes in deep, well-watered but well-drained soil that is richly fertilised and non-alkaline, and at a high altitude, often above 6000 ft (1800 m). It also likes warmth, mist and breeze. The subcontinent provides these conditions in three primary regions: on the western slopes of the hills of Sri Lanka, in the Western Ghats in south-west India, and in the foothills of the Himalayas, notably in the valleys draining into the Brahmaputra, where monsoon rains and daily temperatures of 95°F (35°C) create a natural hothouse. In Assam, which has more than 2000 estates, conditions are particularly favourable.

Tea bushes are kept at a height of about 5 ft (1.5 m), so they can be picked by hand. They produce two to four harvests a year. The flavours and aromas of teas depend on the quality of the soil, the maturity of the leaves and the way they are processed after picking.

The success of English tea

In 1823 Robert Bruce discovered wild tea bushes growing in Assam. Ten years later, with his brother Charles Alexander, he made his first harvest. But Britain owes its dominant role in the tea trade to botanist Robert Fortune, who during the 1850s acclimatised Chinese plants in India and Ceylon.

Along the spice route

Spices were a treasured commodity in the Mediterranean world in ancient times, but their source remained a mystery. Two centuries after Marco Polo reached the spice ports on the south-western coast of India, the Portuguese – followed by other European powers – made a bid to control this lucrative trade and altered the course of history in the subcontinent.

Hot stuff *A sackful of chillies.*

After his discovery of the Malabar Coast, Marco Polo wrote: 'There is in this kingdom a great quantity of pepper, ginger, cinnamon, turbith [a root used in medicine] and coconut', revealing the source of these valuable commodities that reached the Mediterranean only through Arab intermediaries.

Flower power *The crocuses of Kashmir are a major source of saffron.*

Food for thought
Cardamom pods are sorted and graded by hand. The shells contain pungent seeds, celebrated for their complex aroma as well as for their medicinal properties, as a digestive and in treating heart complaints.

The power of spices

Spices were treasured not so much as food flavourings, but for their antiseptic and medicinal properties. They were thought to help combat tropical infections, scurvy and cholera; to stimulate the stomach and the intestines; and to have diuretic and tonic properties. They were used to preserve meat and to make perfumes, and were ascribed various magical and mystical powers.

In the 14th century the Italian missionary monk Oderic of Pordenone witnessed the cultivation of pepper – then a precious spice greatly valued since Roman times – during a voyage to the Malabar Coast: 'They place the pepper plants next to trees, as we do with vines, and pepper grows in bunches like grapes … but when the seeds are ripe they are green.'

It was the Venetian merchant Niccolo di Conti who discovered the cinnamon tree in Ceylon in the next century: 'This tree is like a willow, but taller, and its branches spread out more. The bark on the branches is better and more delicate than that of the trunk.' Spurred by such reports, Henry 'the Navigator' (1394-1460), Prince

Warm and wet *Pepper vines fare best in areas of high rainfall, such as the Cardamom and Nilgiri Hills of the Western Ghats, where the rainy season lasts from March to November.*

of Portugal, set his sights on securing this trade for Portugal and became an important patron for expeditions and research into geography, navigation and sea routes. In 1495 Vasco da Gama was appointed leader of an expedition charged with finding the sea route to the Indies via the southern tip of Africa. He reached Calicut on May 20, 1498, after a journey of 10 months and returned home in triumph bearing samples of spices – but 115 members of his crew of 170 had perished in the enterprise.

Pedros Cabral took up the challenge and reached Calicut in 1500 (having stumbled across Brazil on the way). He set up a Portuguese 'factory' to trade in spices, but after he left, the factory was burned and the Portuguese staff were slaughtered. Vasco da Gama volunteered to lead a fleet to avenge this loss and to seize the monopoly in shipping in spices from the Muslim Arabs. He set sail with some 20 warships and bombarded Calicut with cannon, before making a treaty with the ruler of the rival port of Cochin. In October 1502 his ships were loaded for the return journey with gems, cloth and tons of spices – including so much pepper that it depressed European prices by 50 per cent.

Spices, then, were the lure that brought the Europeans to India. The Portuguese were the first to establish permanent trading ports in the subcontinent. They were followed by the Dutch, who took over the cinnamon

The pepper vine

trade in Ceylon (Sri Lanka remains the world's largest producer of cinnamon). The French and the English arrived in their turn, trading spices and then acquiring land to create their own plantations.

Pepper, the 'king of spices'

Pepper came originally from the hills and forests of Kerala, where it thrives in the hot, humid climate. The word is believed to derive from the Sanskrit *pippali*. In the wild, pepper is a vine that roots itself in the limbs of trees. It produces bunches of green berries which, when picked and dried, become the familiar black peppercorns. Berries left on the vines redden as they mature. These can be used as red pepper, or soaked, shelled and dried to make white pepper.

In ideal conditions, a plantation can grow some 1000 pepper vines per acre (2500 per hectare), and each vine can produce 4.5–6.5 lb (2–3 kg) of pepper every year for 10–30 years. The vines grow best on natural supports, such as mango, kapok or jackfruit trees, where they benefit from the shade of the leaf canopy. The quality, flavour and aroma depend on the soil, climate and plant type. As with wine, there are good and less good vintages for pepper.

Ginger from the Malabar Coast was famous even in ancient times, and the world's best ginger today is said to be found in the old Jewish quarter of Cochin, in Kerala. The dockside warehouses of this region are heady with the mingled scents of exotic spices – of cardamom, cumin, coriander, chillies, turmeric, galangal, mustard seeds, onion seeds, nutmeg and mace, tamarind, star aniseed, fenugreek, saffron and cloves.

Ginger snap Salesmen await their clients in a shop specialising in the trade and export of ginger.

Chillies and pepper

The British sahib in the days of the Raj prided himself on his ability to stomach really hot curries and demanded that everything should be very hot. But this obsession with spicy heat is not typically Indian. Most Indian cuisine is about subtlety of flavour, not the ability to deliver pain. Chillies were introduced by the Portuguese after the Spanish discovery of the Americas (where chillies originally come from) in the 16th century. Prior to that, the fiery heat in Indian cooking came from black pepper and mustard seeds.

Precision *An engraved emerald from the Mughal period.*

A treasury of diamonds and precious stones

Southern Asia's rich seams of gems attracted and fascinated the rich and powerful in antiquity, and gave rise to tales of the glittering wealth of the Mughal emperors and later maharajas. Many of the mines have been exhausted, but the legacy of their wealth can still be admired in the jewels displayed in many of the world's greatest museums.

Legend has it that Alexander the Great wanted to visit a diamond mine, but the entrance was blocked by serpents whose gaze could deal instant death. Alexander devised a cunning plan to trick them: he handed out mirrors to those accompanying him, and when the serpents saw their own reflections, they died on the spot. The seam where the diamonds lay was at the bottom of a deep hole, so Alexander thought up another ruse. He ordered his men to slaughter a sheep and to throw pieces of meat into the hole. Vultures then flew down into the hole, and when they flew out again, the pieces of meat held in their talons were encrusted with diamonds. The men simply had to chase the vultures away to gather a rich harvest.

The marvels of Golconda

This story gives some indication of the treasures that were associated with India in the distant past – and its reputation for riches was not unfounded. The name of Golconda, an ancient city near Hyderabad, in the Deccan, was linked with diamonds and other gems for many centuries. It evoked dreams of fabulous treasures – princes covered in jewels riding on saddles encrusted with glittering stones. The throne of the Nizam al-Mulk of Hyderabad was decorated with 100 rubies of between 100 and 200 carats. The famous Koh-i-Noor diamond is said by some to have come from Golconda.

All invaders were attracted by the reputation of the fabulous riches of the Deccan. It was the Asian Eldorado. In the 4th century BC, Chandragupta, the founder of the Mauryan Empire, became the first sovereign to enrich the Indian royal treasury with precious stones, and to control trade in them. The Muslim conquerors of the 13th and 14th centuries were equally hungry for gems: the Khalje and Tughluq dynasties, who controlled the Sultanate of Delhi, repeatedly launched incursions into the Deccan in pursuit of more treasure.

The ancient Egyptians, Persians, Greeks and Romans all coveted these precious stones, and were prepared to pay handsome sums to merchants who brought them. In Europe precious stones were for many centuries the sole preserve of kings and the Church. But at the end of the Middle Ages, nobles and rich merchants were able to enter the market, just as European gem-cutting and polishing

Treasure-trove *The basket of a Sri Lankan miner may contain gems such as sapphires and rubies. The three largest blue sapphires in the world were all found on the island.*

became a more precise art. Thus when the Portuguese, followed by the Dutch, set up their trading posts in India, they were not after spices alone, but also precious stones. As a result of this long-standing tradition of export, many of India's gemstones are scattered worldwide. All that remains of Golconda are the 16th and 17th century tombs of the Kutb Shahi kings and the ruins of their huge fortress; the mines that it protected have long since been exhausted. India now produces very few diamonds: only the mine at Panna is still in operation.

The trade goes on

India has recently re-entered the diamond market. Surat in Gujarat has become a world centre for cutting and polishing tiny imported diamonds that were previously judged too small to turn into jewels. Emeralds, on which the Mughals engraved verses of the Koran, are mined in the upper reaches of the Indus and in Rajasthan.

Gem-mining still plays an important role in the economy of Sri Lanka. Ratnapura, in the south-west of the island, is the 'gem centre': it has the world's largest sapphire seam and is also the source of rubies, garnets,

Going, going This rare and precious 17th-century necklace was put up for auction in a sale of Indian jewellery mounted by Christie's of London in 1997.

topaz, zircons and beryls. These are found in the gravel-bearing strata that are often mined and sorted using the traditional method of washing then sifting the gravel in baskets.

Gems are still prized in Southern Asian culture, not only as items of jewellery, but as symbols of love, fertility and hope. They are believed to have cosmic powers that influence the destiny of the wearer.

The curse of the Koh-i-noor

It may not be the biggest diamond in the world, but the Koh-i-Noor is certainly the most famous. The French traveller Jean-Baptiste Tavernier, seeing it at the court of the Mughal Emperor Aurangzeb at the end of the 17th century, compared its 280-carat size to an egg, and called it 'the Great Mughal'. Re-cut to just 108 carats, the stone was renamed Koh-i-Noor: 'Mountain of Light'. It is said to carry this curse: 'He who owns this diamond will own the world but will also know all its misfortunes. Only God or a woman can wear it with impunity.' It was owned by a string of Persian and Afghan sovereigns whose reigns all ended in tragedy. Then it came to the Maharaja Duleep Singh of the Punjab, who gave it to Queen Victoria.
It is now in the crown worn by the late Queen Elizabeth the Queen Mother at her coronation in 1937.

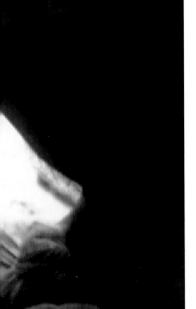

Valuable work Intense concentration reigns in a jewellery workshop in India. The importance of the industry is a reflection of the fact that jewellery is a status symbol.

The quest for energy

One of the greatest economic problems for India is its energy shortage. While its industries soar, the production of electricity has plateaued. The recent discovery of more offshore reserves of natural gas takes away some of the pressure to find new sources of energy – but only in the short term. India has to continue to look for solutions to match the growing expectations and demands of its people.

Running on empty *Women in Bangalore protest against a price-hike for kerosene, the fuel most commonly used for cooking and heating water.*

The inadequacies of India's energy supply may not place the Indian economy under immediate threat, but it does pose awkward questions about lost potential. With depressing regularity, the vast Indian ports and the ten million pumps vital for field irrigation are brought to a standstill by power cuts. Every year the losses caused by the shortfall in energy run into billions of dollars.

Developing a feasible energy strategy

According to the Paris-based International Energy Agency, 43 per cent of India's population – nearly 437 million people – had electricity in 2000. All towns now have electricity, as well as 487 000 villages out of a total of 579 000 (against only 5000 with electricity in 1950), but not all the houses in those villages have a supply.

About three-quarters of India's electricity is generated by coal- and oil-fired power stations, 23 per cent comes from hydroelectric plants, and 3 per cent is generated at India's nine nuclear plants. Hydroelectricity may seem the best solution for such a mountainous country and a major hydroelectric network is being developed in the foothills of the Himalayas. But the creation of dams and power stations has proved highly complex in terms of logistics, strategic implications and infrastructure maintenance, as well as having an ecological impact. The Ganges, for example, is not only sacred, but a crucial source of irrigation, and also a temperamental river, hard to control.

The riches of the deep

At the start of the 1980s, the discovery of oil reserves in the Arabian Sea engendered a wave of optimism. But India produces only about three-fifths of the oil and petrol it consumes. Imported oil creates a big hole in its balance of payments, and predictions suggest that its oil wells will soon be exhausted. Vast reserves of natural gas have been found off the west and south-west coasts, but this runs far short of supplying the nation's energy needs in the long term.

For well over 100 years, scientists and inventors have been trying to exploit one renewable and cheap resource that Southern Asia has in bountiful quantities: sunshine. To date, solar energy has found practical use only in small-scale projects, but a technological breakthrough may lie in the future.

Natural energy *Solar panels recharge the batteries in a lantern.*

Ecological fault *The Narmada Dam project has been opposed both by local people it affects and by activists concerned about the ecological impact.*

The exotic bazaar

There are many reasons why tourists come to India: for relaxation, for the culture, to trek in the hills or climb the mountains, to search for eternal truths. With its extraordinary contrasts and extremes, India never fails to surprise, and the experiences of visitors often exceed all expectations.

Spiritual quest *Westerners come in search of Eastern philosophy, as at this yoga school in the northern state of Bihar.*

About 2.5 million foreigners visit India every year – a comparatively small number by international standards, placing it at around 45th in the 'most-visited countries' rankings. But this is nonetheless an impressive figure, given that India is not considered an 'easy' country to visit. More than anything, a visit to India presents a cultural challenge to Westerners: the teeming streets, the profusion of colours and architectural styles, and the many varying languages, castes and religions can make trying to understand India something of a challenge; but there are many rewards for those who persevere.

A road well travelled

Some people come to India to relive the myth of the hippie trail along the famous beaches of Goa, on the west coast of India. As the sun goes down over the Arabian Sea, crowds of young Westerners gyrate to the throb of techno music. Trekking is a popular form of escape: small groups follow their guides along the remote mountain trails in Ladakh and Zanskar or Himachal Pradesh.

Others come in search of spiritual enlightenment. There are thousands of ashrams – places where a spiritual master dispenses his teachings to his disciples. Some are places of deep prayer and self-denial (*srama* in Sanskrit means 'religious exertion'); others are devoted to charitable works and education.

For many, the real highlights of India are its famous architectural and cultural marvels, such as the Taj Mahal, the temples of Khajuraho, and the murals of the Ajanta Caves. These are just some of the best-known examples – every region has scores of sites of

religious, architectural or historical significance. These places are not reserved for foreigners: the great sights are often actively used by local people, and an increasing number of Indians are also taking advantage of their growing disposable income to discover their own heritage.

Sherpas: essential guides

Think of Himalayan mountain guides and the word Sherpa springs to mind. The centre of the Sherpa world lies in the Khumbu and Solu regions of northern Nepal, close to the border with Tibet. In the past these tough mountain people lived by farming their unforgiving landscape and carrying salt across the mountains to trade for rice. Numbering some 35 000 today, many have found new careers in tourism, as guides and camp staff. Speaking broken English interspersed with Nepali and their own dialect, more than half now live off this trade. At the start of each climbing season, they set up the high-altitude camps and haul equipment up to them, notably oxygen. The porters can walk for 8–10 hours a day carrying loads of 70 lb (32 kg). About 20 per cent of the 750 or so people who have reached the summit of Everest have been Sherpas. One name stands out: Tenzing Norgay, who with the New Zealander Edmund Hillary, was the first to conquer Everest in 1953.

Joint effort *Sherpas cross a raging torrent on Mount Manaslu, Nepal.*

Cultural heritage *The Taj Mahal, in Agra, receives about 10 million visitors a year, the vast majority of them Indian.*

More than a billion souls

If it had not divided into three at Partition, India, Pakistan and Bangladesh would today form the most populous country in the world. As it is, India is ranked second in the world after China, but it has a much higher birth-rate, and is predicted to overtake China by 2050, when its total population may reach 1.5 billion.

Public information *Mobile family planning units offer advice and help.*

In May 2000, hospital guards used batons to hold back a crowd of 200 journalists and photographers who had descended on a Delhi hospital to witness the arrival of India's 'billionth baby' – the moment when the population supposedly hit the one billion mark. It was a fairly arbitrary guess: in India a baby is born every two seconds – a total of 17 million births a year, the equivalent of the entire population of Australia. But the interest was significant: this was yet another indicator that India's population is spiralling upwards and putting a relentless strain on resources. Public health initiatives and preventative medicine, as well as the receding threat of famine and epidemics, have resulted in a tripling of the population since independence in 1947.

Families have an average of three children. With infant mortality now comparatively low, one-third of the population is under 15. And people are living longer: life expectancy for both men and women is about 64 years.

Combating growth

The Indian government has tried to limit population growth through birth control. In 1951 India was one of the first nations in the world to introduce a family planning programme as a central priority of government. But between 1975 and 1977 Prime Minister Indira Gandhi waged a campaign of forced sterilisation, a deeply unpopular policy that affected nearly 4.5 million men and undermined the work of family planning doctors working in local communities.

Since then, the Indian State has refused to impose any birth control policies. In its favour, one can argue that this decision respects human rights and avoids any possibility of birth control being used to promote one or other ethnic or religious group. The government is nonetheless encouraging couples to limit their families to just two children. Instead of sterilisation, however, it proposes the use of simple and conventional birth control methods, such as the coil. Mobile family planning units regularly travel the country to promote their services and to give advice. Generally, families do take advantage of what the units have to offer, once they have acquired the number of children they desire – but this is often well in excess of two.

City life *Crowds throng the streets of Jaipur, capital of Rajasthan, a city of nearly 2 million people.*

Family ties *A courtyard in Delhi shows the cramped conditions in which many people live. Delhi (population 11.7 million) is India's third largest city.*

Varied fortunes of Southern Asia's diaspora

An estimated 20 million Southern Asians live outside the subcontinent, the result of a migratory movement that began in colonial times. More than 850 000 Indians, 350 000 Pakistanis and 120 000 Bangladeshis live in Britain. Over half the people in Fiji and 40 per cent in Trinidad are of Indian origin.

New life in a new land Mr and Mrs Mohammadi, formerly citizens of Pakistan, proudly show their new allegiance to the Stars and Stripes, having just been granted their American citizenship.

During the 19th century, successive waves of Indians left their homeland for other British colonies in Africa, the West Indies and the islands of the South Pacific. Gradually they spread to almost all parts of the world, forming communities of Indians, Bangladeshis, Pakistanis and Sri Lankans. In these new lands they founded businesses that were sometimes very successful, but often more modest. Or they worked as labourers and servants, as many still do in the Gulf states.

Diaspora: an aid to development
In the 1960s, a generation of trained professionals – doctors, engineers and entrepreneurs – chose to pursue their careers in richer countries, often with noted success. In the USA, for example, the Indian community is one of the most prosperous ethnic groups, while in the UK some Indian businessmen rank among the most wealthy in the country.

At home in Britain Young Muslim Pakistanis can benefit from an upbringing that is part British and part Asian.

For many years, successive governments of India have refused to pay much heed to this diaspora. Until the late 1980s the economic principles established by Nehru still held sway: protectionism and the philosophy of *swadeshi* or 'Indian goods for India' (that is, minimal imports). But the liberalising economic reforms launched by the government in 1991 began to acknowledge the potential represented by this émigré community, who could promote foreign investment in a pattern similar to that of China, whose diaspora has made a major contribution to China's economic development. Since then, investment from the Indian diaspora has flooded in, seen particularly in property, in hospitals and in the textile industry. As it turns out, many émigrés have remained loyal to 'Mother India' and are keen to renew their bonds.

Not such a rosy picture
Businessmen from Southern Asia are among Britain's richest millionaires, but this doesn't mean that all Asians are prospering in Britain. Following race riots in northern cities in the summer of 2001, surveys found that more than 75 per cent of Asians live in households with an income below the national average; the unemployment rate for adult males was 2.5 times higher than the national average, and wages of those in work was 65 per cent lower. Many live in overcrowded houses in poor conditions and suffer regular racial harassment in the streets.

New land, old traditions Replicating a ritual from their homeland, Hindus pull a float dedicated to Ganesha, the elephant-headed god, through the streets of Paris.

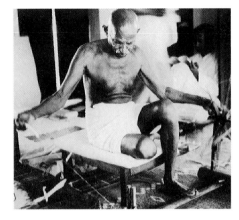

From the spinning wheel to the electronic mouse

One of the most surprising contrasts in India is that of technology: the obsolete co-exists with the most sophisticated – a reflection of a society where luxury jostles with extreme poverty, and where a two-speed economy produces consumer goods of extraordinary disparity.

Self-sufficient *Gandhi spinning (1946).*

Mahatma Gandhi used the spinning wheel as a symbol of the struggle for Indian independence: the call to Indians to wear clothes spun and woven by hand signified a return to the country's origins and a refusal to rely on Western methods to supply their needs. But, to a degree this return to basics was misleading, obscuring an ancient tradition of intellectual and scientific excellence, which had until the 18th century made India technologically more advanced than the West. And at the time of Gandhi, many Indians were working hard to redress the balance.

Top scientist *Chandrasekhara Raman (1888-1970) won the Nobel prize for physics in 1930.*

New nuclear powers

The scion of a leading Parsee family from Bombay, atomic scientist Homi Bhabha pursued a brilliant academic career at Cambridge, where he worked with Neils Bohr and Ernest Rutherford, pioneers of nuclear physics. He returned to India in 1939 to take up a post as Special Reader in Theoretical Physics at the Indian Institute of Science at Bangalore, before moving to the Tata Institute of Fundamental Research in Mumbai (Bombay) in 1945. After independence, he led the government

nuclear research programme which in 1956 created India's first nuclear reactor. Today, India's nuclear energy programme plays a vital role in the nation's electricity supply, helping to compensate for the low reserves in coal.

Although the Tata Institute is dedicated to the peaceful use of atomic power, this work had strategic implications. On May 18, 1974, India carried out its first underground nuclear bomb test in the Thar Desert. On May 11 and 13, 1998, five further tests permitted the prime minister, head of a Hindu national government, to declare that 'India is now a nuclear power.' Two weeks later, Pakistan tested six atomic bombs, to the joy of supporters who proclaimed 'Glory to the Islamic bomb', and increased the stakes in the ongoing enmity between the two countries.

Information technology

Backed by its numerous prestigious institutions, India has the second largest scientific community in the world after the USA, and leading Indian scientists are constantly being solicited by American research laboratories, businesses and hospitals. The information revolution owes much to India: through modern telecommunications, the two leading hi-tech cities in India, Bangalore and Hyderabad, make their know-how and facilities available to the rest of the world

Wheels of time *A woman spins cotton in Rajasthan. Gandhi sided with craft-based, non-industrial village traditions, in contrast to Nehru, a socialist and modernist, whose vision prevailed.*

The Tata family: industry and philanthropy

The Tata family have played a key role in the development of industry in India. Jamsetji Tata founded his first textile mill in Nagpur in 1877; in 1901 he built a large-scale iron foundry, and in 1907 inaugurated a steel mill in the new town of Jamshedpur in Bihar, which he built close to the ore and coal mines. Tata was an enlightened industrialist, paying great attention to the working conditions of his employees, and setting up a pension fund and an accident compensation scheme. The family founded the Indian Institute of

Sciences at Bangalore in 1911, and the Tata Institute of Fundamental Research at Bombay (or National Centre for Nuclear Science and Mathematics) in 1945, as well as three other major institutes. They have set up trusts that fund educational, social and healthcare institutions, and promote scientific and artistic teaching and practice. The Tata family still controls a holding company that owns a diversified group of businesses, including heavy industries, power plants, and factories producing chemicals, hi-tech and other goods.

Visions of the future An employee inspects circuits at Micropack, in Bangalore – the city that has been dubbed India's Silicon Valley.

at low-cost. For identical levels of competence, engineers are paid ten times more in the USA. This very rapid development in information technology is the cause of some strange contrasts: computers used to monitor stock flicker among heaps of spices in a warehouse, or sit on desks in banks beside large handwritten registers interleaved with carbon paper and piles of worn bank-notes.

In touch with the modern world *Under the slogan 'Banking for the Poor', the Grameen Bank offers loans without collateral to Bangladeshi villagers. It has also sprouted a family of philanthropic enterprises, such as Grameen Telecom, which finances the provision of mobile phones.*

CHAPTER 3

LIVING ON THE SUBCONTINENT

The difficult challenge facing countries in Southern Asia today is how to live together in mutual tolerance, without a unifying language or religion, and with gaping inequalities. The people have a natural resilience and an inherited ability to play the long game. With each new wave of invaders, the people of the subcontinent showed their adaptability. They took what they wanted from the new values imposed upon them, and over time diffused the impact of invasion. A religious perspective plays its part. The Hindus and Buddhists have *dharma*, the right way of living in the sacred order of the world; Muslims surrender to the will of Allah. But there are deep divides between the religious and ethnic groups. Inter-communal and inter-ethnic disputes all too often flare up into violence, which threatens the political stability of the region and undermines efforts to tackle the day-to-day problems of chronic underdevelopment.

Ablutions in the Narmada, a river in western India held sacred by the Hindus.

The caste system

The Portuguese were the first to use the word 'caste' in the 15th century, to describe the social organisation of the Indian people. It provides the essential structure of the Hindu world – both now and in the afterlife.

According to the Hindu text, the *Rig Veda*, the human world was created when the gods dismembered the cosmic body, conceived in the image of man, and offered it in sacrifice. The mouth became the Brahmans (or Brahmins), the priestly caste; the warriors came from the shoulders and arms; the merchants and artisans came from the thighs, and the servants from the feet.

Class and caste

Struggling to define this social system, Portuguese missionaries had recourse to the Latin *castus*, which means pure. They understood that Indian society was divided into an upper stratum of 'pure' occupations and the lower echelons who did 'impure' jobs. But this was an oversimplification. When the Aryan tribes arrived in the subcontinent 3500 years ago, they brought with them a system that divided society into four *varnas* (in Sanskrit the word means 'colour'). The Brahmans stood at the pinnacle of the social hierarchy as they were the priests and the most pure. As with all the *varnas*, however, the roles are now more loosely defined. Today,

Purification   *A Brahman bathes in the River Ganges at Varanasi.*

Lowly work *This family of tanners is considered impure, and hence 'casteless', on account of its work with leather.*

Caste: a thing of the past?

The Indian Constitution of 1950 rejected all discrimination based on religion, race, caste, gender or place of birth. A quota policy gave the Untouchables, or *dalits*, access to professions from which they had previously been barred, but these quotas have been widely ignored. Often accused of transgressing tradition, the *dalits* are still victims of disputes, murder and rape. Hinduism in India has recently taken a swing toward conservatism; a reaction against attempts to modernise by breaking down social barriers and focusing on individual merit. Non-Hindu *dalits* in particular have been the victims of extremists. Meanwhile, the government of Nepal has announced plans to out-law caste discrimination in an attempt to address long-standing grievances of Nepalese *dalits*.

Equality of opportunity *In 1997, Kocheril Raman Narayanan became the first Untouchable to be appointed President of India.*

It is difficult for Westerners to accept a form of social organisation that does not embrace the concept of equality for everyone, but in the Hindu religion inequality is not seen as injustice, but as part of the order of the Universe.

many Brahmans are landowners, or professionals working in administration, business or teaching. A large number are also cooks, because only a Brahman can cook for another Brahman, many of whom are vegetarian.

The Kshatriya are the second social group. In the past, they were the princes, warriors and administrators, but today they are found in a broad range of occupations. The third class, the Vaisya, have remained closer to their original job definition and tend to be arti-sans, craftworkers, farmers and merchants. Only the men of these three upper or 'pure' *varnas* have the right to sport the 'sacred thread', which is worn from the left shoulder and tied on the right hip. This is given at an initiation rite considered as a second birth, and so these castes are also referred to as the 'twice-born' (*dvija*).

At the bottom of the *varna* hierarchy are the Sudra, the 'servants', who make up the vast majority of the Indian population. Although considered impure, and capable of 'polluting' those from higher *varnas*, they are not Untouchables. Most remain within their orig-inal role, providing services for the higher castes.

Untouchability

The Untouchables are those without caste – called *harijans*, or 'Children of God', by Gandhi. Originally they were the non-Aryans, obliged to do the most lowly work – grave-diggers, sweepers and knackers. They are still locked into this low status. Considered impure by the higher castes, and capable of spreading pollution, they have to respect traditions of segregation. Also grouped with them are the tribal peoples, as well as the religious minorities (Muslims, Sikhs, Christians). The Untouchables and tribal groups are often also known as *dalit*, the oppressed.

Over time, the additional classification, *jati*, has been grafted onto the ancient social order of the *varnas*. The *jatis* are defined by occupation (usually a hereditary profession), and the degrees of purity associated with that occupation; they are also defined by location, such as a group of villages. There are numerous *jatis* within each *varna*. Their taboos – for example, against marriage to, even eating with, members of other *jatis* – are strictly observed, especially in rural areas.

Caste conflict

The social hierarchies of *varna* and *jati* persist because they are an inalienable part of the Hindu religion, an essential order. Class and caste are inherited at birth and immutable in this life. It is useless, even dangerous, to rebel against this order. Those that cross caste boundaries risk rejection from their communities, even violent retribution. Caste prejudices and poverty were key moti-vations in the criminal life of the 'Bandit Queen' Phoolan Devi, an outlaw of low-caste origins, and later a member of parliament. She was killed in 2001, aged 37, by an upper-caste assassin, in a dra-matic tale of cross-caste rape, vengeance and slaughter.

Eternal order *During the Kumbha Mela festival, a Brahman family carries out rituals at Trimbak, the source of the sacred River Godavari. Note the sacred cords worn across the shoulders of several of the men.*

Love luck *A fortune-teller's advert in Madras promises clairvoyance in matters of the heart. Before marriage, couples often consult palmists or astrologers to check compatibility.*

The price of marriage

The vast majority of India's hugely popular movies are based on love and romance. But, in reality, most marriages are arranged by the families involved. This applies particularly to Hindus, who must observe caste barriers, but arranged marriage is also practised by Muslims.

Thousands of 'matrimonial classifieds' for both men and women appear daily in India, in newspapers and now increasingly on the Internet: 'Female, 26, 5 ft 3 in (160 cm). Never married. Religion: Hindu-Vaisya. Culture: Malayalee. Occupation: IT/Computer. Location: India. I have an IT job in the Ministry of Defence. Father retired central government officer, having one daughter and two sons. Mother is a housewife. Two brothers self-employed. Seeking alliance with suitable family. Ad Code: 214178'. Adverts such as this reflect two key trends in Indian matchmaking. First, that most marriages are conducted along carefully selective lines, based on religion, caste, ethnic background, status and economic class. Second, that young Indians find it extremely difficult to meet suitable partners in the course of daily life. The concept of dating is virtually unknown.

Arranged marriages

Until recently very young children were assigned to marriages, a practice that is now illegal and punishable, although impossible to eradicate entirely. Adult marriages arranged by the parents, however, are perfectly legal and indeed the norm among many groups, not just Hindu, but also Muslim, Buddhist and even Christian,

especially in the upper echelons of society, where the preservation of status within the family is extremely important. Among poorer families, a huge premium is placed on choosing the right match for different reasons. In countries were there is no social security, people can look only to their families for some level of comfort in illness, misfortune and old age, particularly in the countryside, where unemployment is widespread.

Society in Southern Asia is organised around the extended family, which brings together under one roof father, mother, grandparents, uncles and unmarried aunts. Women selected for arranged marriages with the sons of the family have to fit into this tight-knit community, and so the marriage is considered to be the property of this extended family, not just of the individuals who marry one another. Aunts are key players in finding suitable candidates for an arranged marriage. If no suitable candidate emerges, the family will start looking through the matrimonial classifieds, or seek the help of a marriage broker.

Often such unions are arranged with speed and the couple may hardly know each other when they marry, but in modern cities and among the middle classes, arranged marriages are increasingly made with the consent of the couple. Even then, marriages rarely

The dowry: an enduring tradition

India's Constitution forbids the practice of offering a dowry at marriage, but the tradition has not died out. The family of the groom receives presents from the family of the bride, as a good match is considered worth the price. Parents want to see their daughters well married: the richer the family, the easier it will be for them to secure a good husband for the daughter. The size of the dowry is negotiated according to the social rank, the net worth and the occupation of the fiancé. Dowries can be the cause of debt, adding to the financial burden of the wedding.

Blessings on bride and groom *An officiating Brahman conducts the rituals at a marriage ceremony in Bangalore.*

New generation   A young woman proudly carries her child in Jaisalmer, Rajasthan. In the past, girls would be married before reaching puberty. Today they cannot marry before the age of 14, while the husband must be at least 18.

cross community or caste barriers, except among very Westernised families. If a self-selecting young couple resolutely choose to brazen out family disapproval, they will be subjected to all kinds of pressure, such as the threat of expulsion from the family home, being disinherited, and being held responsible for bringing shame to the family. Hopeless love matches are one of the favourite themes of Indian and Pakistani films, and they always end badly.

Women in the home

The dowry plays a major role in marriage, so the birth of a son is greeted with more joy than that of a girl. The son can perpetuate the family line, provide for the parents in their dotage, and see the correct rituals are performed at their death. A daughter holds no guarantees for the future: she will leave home, and her dowry will be a burden. During childhood, girls receive less attention than boys – which explains why infant mortality is higher for girls than for boys. India has 106 men for every 100 women (in Europe and the USA there are marginally more women than men).

Working women   Low-paid manual labour is the lot of many women in India. Here they build an embankment for a railway line, near Madurai in Tamil Nadu.

Southern Asia has a complex attitude towards women. The married woman is idealised as the central figure in the home. But the image of the woman as the devoted guardian of her household does not represent the whole truth. Women play a key role in the workplace – in the fields, on building sites, in schools, offices and public life. Tradition dictates that widows do not remarry. In the past, some high-caste Hindu women would perform *sati*, throwing themselves on their husband's funeral pyre, though this was never as widespread as is often supposed.

Hinduism: guiding the soul from one life to the next

Hinduism is founded on two central principles: the transmigration of souls through a cycle of rebirths and the law of karma *– the concept that actions in this life will determine one's fate in the next. But there is no central orthodoxy, no official Church or centralised authority, and no single book – as exists for the monotheistic religions – to define Hinduism. It is, rather, a broad collection of philosophies and beliefs that encompasses many types of devotion, worship and rituals.*

Hinduism is a tradition that is at once both cultural and religious. It is closely tied to the history of India, and to the way people live and perceive their role in society. All is interconnected with a view of the cosmos, from the creation to eternity, and the way that every individual fits into the order of the Universe.

The guiding principle of human life is reincarnation: everyone is involved in a cycle of rebirths. The main aim in life is to attain merit, under the principle of punishment and reward according to conduct (*karma*), while respecting the law of the harmony and the order of the Universe and one's place in it (*dharma*). Disrespect for *dharma* disturbs the entire cosmic order: sickness, bad harvests or even natural disasters may result. It is therefore essential to respect social order, to practise non-violence and fairness, and to avoid envy and cruelty.

The law of *karma* states that in life there is no such thing as chance. Everything has a cause and effect: every action entails a reaction, from which nothing can escape. The destiny of every individual is determined by one's *karma*, and the life that one leads is the product of former lives. Thus the soul (*atman*) transmigrates and will be endlessly reincarnated, until release (*moksha*) from the cycle of rebirth is achieved, bringing eternal bliss.

According to the theory of the transmigration of souls, *samsara*, the soul can be reincarnated in the body of any other living creature – gods and demons as well as animals, or even bacteria. Any action that goes against the law can lead to punishment, such as being reborn as a lowly insect. But a life in which good *karma* is accumulated by merit can result in an improved status, such as a higher caste, in the next life.

All forms of life should be respected, because they all belong to the system of rebirth. This concept gave rise to the doctrine of *ahimsa*, 'not to harm or injure'. Thus during the 1st millennium AD the sacrifice of animals, which had been practised during Vedic times, was phased out. However, goats are still sacrificed in Calcutta during the festival held in honour of the goddess Kali.

The many gods

Along with the *Veda* ('sacred knowledge') and their caste system, the Aryans brought their gods – Varuna, Vishnu, Agni, Indra, Vrita – to India when they invaded 3500 years ago. These were added to the pantheon of gods already worshipped locally, such as the Mother Goddess – who evolved into the Hindu gods Parvati and Durga. The best-known gods in the Hindu pantheon are Brahma, Vishnu

Lord of the dance *One of the manifestations of Shiva is Shiva Nataraja, Lord of the Dance, seen here in a bronze sculpture dating from the 2nd century AD.*

In all her glory *Devotees around a statue of Durga during the festival of Dussehra or Durga Puja, held to mark the end of the monsoon.*

and Shiva, who form a trinity (*Trimurti*). Brahma, creator of the Universe, is represented seated on a lotus flower, with his four heads turned towards the four horizons, and four arms, one of which holds the primordial water. His vehicle is a wild goose or swan, symbols of purity, and his consort is Sarasvati, goddess of learning.

Vishnu is the preserver of the Universe, and embodiment of kindness and compassion. One of his four hands holds the wheel of destiny. Travelling on Garuda, the white eagle with a human head, he comes down to the human world to re-establish the order of the Universe. He manifests himself in the form of one of his ten avatars (visible forms, or incarnations). The best known of these avatars are Krishna (a hero and ruler who is said to have composed the great eve-of-battle poem the *Bhagavad Gita*); Rama, king and hero of the epic the *Ramayana*; the Buddha; the fish called Matsya; and the tortoise Kurma. His consort is Lakshmi, goddess of wealth and prosperity.

Shiva, lord of deliverance, god of a thousand names, is depicted seated on a tiger skin. He holds a trident and observes the reality of the world with his third eye, which also gives him inward vision. Reality consists of opposites: creation and destruction, good and evil, life and death, celibacy and fertility: all lie within his domain, and Shiva has manifestations that represent both extremes. He becomes four-armed Nataraja when he dances in a circle of fire in representation of cosmic energy and serenity and the cycle of destruction and creation. The bull Nandin is his vehicle. Although Shiva is often represented by the phallic lingam symbol, he also appears in feminine forms, which are venerated along with his consort Parvati, full of benevolence, and her other manifestation Durga or Kali, the female warrior and goddess of destruction.

The three members of the *Trimurti* are often held up to be the most important gods in Hinduism. But this is misleading. Most Hindus have their own views on which gods are the most important, and these can range from Shiva and Vishnu (who are widely popular) to obscure local gods who appear to have little to do with the mainstream pantheon. Worship is vital to propitiate the gods and to protect the worshipper from misfortune. During devotions (*puja*) at home or at a temple, and at religious festivals, offerings are made to the gods: flowers, fruit, sweets, incense, money. More intense spiritual experiences may be achieved through meditation, yoga and audiences with a guru (teacher).

A key concept in Hindu worship is *darshan* ('seeing'). By looking at a sacred image (*murti*) a worshipper can receive its *darshan* or

The lingam and the yoni

A phallic symbol of fertility, power and creativity, the lingam is the most common of all religious emblems in India and Nepal. One estimate suggests there are as many as 30 million of them in the subcontinent. Representing the duality of Shiva, they often sit on a receptacle for offerings called the yoni, symbol of femininity, which has a spout that allows libations to flow away. Sexuality and fertility are key elements in the Hindu cosmic view: without regeneration there can be no cycle of life and death, no *karma* and *samsara*. Hindu women sometimes wear lingam amulets to ensure their fertility.

Say it with flowers *Offerings of flowers decorate a statue of Vishnu (left) at the Devi Jagadamba temple at Khajuraho.*

blessing. For this reason, images of the gods play a very important role in Hinduism: they are not just representations, but embodiments of the deity. They are treated with great respect, are given offerings, and sometimes elaborately dressed. In some temples the images are kept in special sanctuaries and only put on view on certain occasions, and access may be restricted to higher castes.

Guru *Disciples show their reverence for the modern guru Sai Baba.*

The Ramayana *and* Mahabharata

The characteristics of the individual Hindu gods are integrated with their mythology. Many of them appear in the great epics of the *Ramayana* and the *Mahabharata*. All Hindus know these stories from earliest childhood, taking from them lessons about how to face the difficulties of life with courage and energy.

Composed from the 3rd century BC, the *Ramayana* consists of 24 000 couplets, supposedly dictated by Brahma to the poet Valmiki. This vivid picture of the human condition tells how Rama, seventh incarnation of Vishnu and son of the King of Ayodhya, wins the hand of the beautiful Princess Sita in an archery competition. As a result of court intrigue, he is sent into exile. He lives as a hermit in the forest, where he is attacked by the thousands of demons of King Ravana, who seizes Sita for his harem, hoping to be able to seduce her. Rama makes an alliance with the king of the monkeys, who lends him his army,

The religions
- ☐ Hinduism
- ☐ Islam
- ☐ Buddhism
- ☐ Sikhism

commanded by Hanuman. Riding Garuda, Rama sets out to conquer Ravana's kingdom. A monumental battle ensues, in which the demons are defeated. Rama kills Ravana and Sita is freed. But Rama now rejects her, as she has been in the house of another man. In despair, Sita attempts to kill herself with fire. But, as a proof of her innocence, the flames spare her. Rama returns to Ayodhya with Sita, where he is anointed king.

The epic of the *Mahabharata*, with its 200 000 lines of verse, has been compared to Homer's *Iliad*. It tells how the 100 Pandava brothers are cheated of their kingdom and enter into war with the clan of the Kaurava brothers. After a huge battle and 12 days of massacres, the Pandava win back their kingdom. This immense poem, composed in about the 2nd century AD, is above all a work of moral instruction, which permeates the text: the duties of kingship, the rules of conduct, religious and metaphysical considerations. The sixth book of the *Mahabharata*, the *Bhagavad Gita*, is considered the gospel of Hinduism. It recounts how Krishna, the eighth incarnation of Vishnu, intervenes on behalf of Arjuna, the leader of the Pandavas. Arjuna, full of compassion for his enemies, hesitates to commit himself to battle. Krishna shows him his duty, or *dharma*, which as a warrior consists of undertaking just wars, because otherwise souls may be destroyed. All action is inevitable: it has to be carried out with disinterest and for the love of Brahma, which is the way to deliverance.

Blessings *Ganesha, the elephant-headed god, bringer of good fortune, is paraded in a procession on the first day of the Ganesha Chaturthi festival in Mumbai (Bombay).*

Ganesha

Among the many Hindu gods, one stands out as universally popular: Ganesha or Ganesh, the god with the head of an elephant and the body of a man. The son of Shiva and Parvati, he was – according to tradition – decapitated by his father in a misunderstanding. Returning from a long trip, Shiva found Parvati with another man, and, failing to recognise his own son, flew into a temper and chopped off his head. Seeing his error, Shiva replaced Ganesha's head with the head of the first animal he encountered, an elephant. Ganesha's wisdom helps him to remove obstacles for people. He is the god of beginnings and inaugurations, and devotees believe that nothing should be undertaken without an invocation to Ganesha; his image is often found on the doors of dwellings and at the entrances to temples.

The power of the word *A Brahman at a temple in Rameswaram, Tamil Nadu, a city of pilgrimage for devotees of Rama.*

Radical Hinduism

The vast majority of the population of India, 82 per cent, are Hindu. In recent years a radical political movement has become increasingly vociferous and powerful. The Bharitiya Janata Party (BJP), which leads the ruling coalition in the Indian government, is a Hindu nationalist movement. But there are also more conservative and fanatical elements, such as the Shiv Sena Party and the VHP (Vishwa Hindu Parishad, World Hindu Organisation). The latter has a violent youth group called the Bajrang Dal, which orchestrates demonstrations and confrontations with Muslims – notably the destruction in 1992 of the mosque at Ayodhya, in Gujarat, built on a site sacred to Rama. Contention, if not violent confrontation, with non-Hindu members of the population is constantly in the news: Muslims, for instance, have recently been under intense pressure to give up eating beef. And in February 2001 the Shiv Sena Party launched violent attacks in Kanpur, in Uttar Pradesh, against those observing St Valentine's Day.

Devotions *At Sonepur, in Bihar, worshippers press towards the temple with offerings of flowers, food and Ganges water.*

Young and old *The temple of Brihadeshwara, in Tanjore in Tamil Nadu, was built in the 9th century AD, and is famous for its sculptures and mural paintings.*

73

The traditions of pilgrimage

Young and old, rich and poor, Hindus travel in their thousands to all parts of India to pay their devotions to temples, to the special shrines of the gods, to the sacred rivers and to the many other sites of pilgrimage, in search of solace and cosmic merit.

Lifetime's work *Such is the religious fervour of the Hindus that they will undertake pilgrimages well into old age.*

Pilgrimage (*yatra*) is a central feature of Hindu practice. Several times in their life, Hindus will undertake long journeys to visit sacred places. There are many thousands of pilgrimage sites (*tirthas*) throughout India. Often located on the bank of a river or stream, or beside the sea, many consist of no more than a natural feature such as a tree, a pool or an oddly-shaped rock that is associated in some way with the gods. Not all are ancient: the site where Gandhi was cremated in 1948, close to the Yamuna River in Delhi, is now a pilgrimage site.

The most important pilgrimage sites are in the seven holy cities: Varanasi (Benares), which is associated with incarnations of Shiva and Vishnu; Haridwar, also on the Ganges, at the foot of the Himalayas; Ayodhya, on the River Gogra, a tributary of the Ganges; Mathura, on the River Yamuna, birthplace of Krishna; Dwarka, where Krishna was king, on the Arabian Sea; Ujjian, in the Vindhya hills; and Kanchipuram, west of Madras, where Shiva is venerated.

One of the most holy pilgrimages takes in the sites at the four cardinal points of India: Badrinath, near the source of the Ganges, Puri in the east, Rameswaram opposite Sri Lanka, and Dwarka in the west. By train, this journey can be completed in about 10 weeks.

Many of the greatest temple complexes have been built at pilgrimage sites, such as the temple of Jagannath (a manifestation of Vishnu) at Puri. They are like small towns, with numerous shrines, lodgings, shops selling refreshments and souvenirs, and many other facilities catering for tens of thousands of pilgrims a day. At the holy site, pilgrims wash, perform *puja*, and present their offerings to the gods – of flowers, fruits, sweet foods and butter, and libations of fresh or fermented milk – often under the direction of a Brahman priest, who performs the rituals for them.

Evaluating merit

Pilgrimage is supposed to be a leveller: all castes stand as equals when bathing in the waters of the pilgrimage sites, and are said to enter eternity during a pilgrimage. The deeds and merit accomplished during life on earth determine an individual's destiny in the next life, and pilgrimage can earn considerable merit. Quite how this is calculated depends on the individual's beliefs: some say that more merit is acquired by walking (rather than by using transport), and the further the better. Timing (to coincide with sacred days in the calendar) and the relative holiness of the pilgrimage site may also be taken into account.

Holy water *Ritual baths are the centrepiece of a Kumbha Mela, a gathering of several million pilgrims, which takes place every three years in one of four holy cities of India.*

The ascetic sadhus

Leading a life of solitary vagabonds, sadhus are part of the Indian landscape. When they are not on their travels, they can often be seen around the temples, at the great pilgrimage centres and at Hindu festivals, such as the Kumbha Mela.

Piercing pain *As part of his strategy for self-mortification, a sadhu in Mysore stands on nails.*

A man lies on a plank pierced with nails; another rejects all human contact and buries his head in sand for several days; another does not speak, having taken a vow of silence. Sadhus will undergo all kinds of endurance tests and acts of self-mortification in their quest to achieve spiritual enlightenment, and many appear to acquire exceptional powers of 'mind-over-body'.

Liberation through self-denial

Convinced that the Universe is based on illusion, or *maya*, sadhus have chosen the path of utter renunciation. Like the gurus, the spiritual teachers of Hinduism, they are in pursuit of the absolute, but in their case the quest is an entirely personal one. They reject any attachment to material things and any participation in economic life. Some begin their careers as sadhus when they are children; others are ordinary men (and also women) who have turned away from conventional society in order to pursue their religious quest through austerity and self-denial.

They hope to free themselves of bad *karma* and to draw nearer to the world of the divine. They are concerned with defeating the ills of egotism, which are the product of desire and illusion. To achieve these ends they may practise yoga, and believe that travelling is essential to keep the spirit active.

Most sadhus have very few possessions apart from their saffron robes, and some, the *naga sadhus*, go about entirely naked and smeared with ash (a symbol of penance). Many are followers of Shiva and are said to present themselves in his image, with their uncut beards and hair, their foreheads marked with three lines of paint, and strings of beads and necklaces. They may also carry symbols of Shiva, such as an iron trident and an hourglass-shaped double-ended drum or *damaru*, beaten to announce their presence. They may also carry a metal jug to hold water for libations, and a goblet or human skull in which to receive offerings of food.

Although impossible to count, it is believed that the total number of sadhus amounts to several million. Considered by ordinary people to be saints, sadhus live on alms, and may not even have to beg, as those who give earn merit by so doing. But some sadhus are charlatans, who exploit the generosity of the public. Those performing feats of bodily endurance may simply be using well-known tricks of illusion, and many have been exposed as frauds.

Material world *Some sadhus, like this one in Gujarat, live in relative, if simple, comfort.*

The teachings of gurus

Gurus are spiritual masters, who live with their disciples in an ashram or a monastery. In the quest for truth, they promote meditation, dietary control and physical disciplines (such as yoga) to achieve the liberation of the soul. Their word can reach millions of devotees, and they may be treated with god-like reverence. Perhaps the best known today is Sai Baba (born 1926), with several million followers – although sceptics dismiss his paranormal powers and miracles as conjuror's illusions.

Naked before God *Sadhus queue for a ritual bath at Kumbha Mela.*

The cradle of Buddhism

Founded in the middle of the 6th century BC, Buddhism was the leading religion of India for more than ten centuries, and spread throughout South-east Asia. Then it all but disappeared from the subcontinent, but it is still the official religion of Sri Lanka and Bhutan, and of many of the remotest regions of the Himalayas.

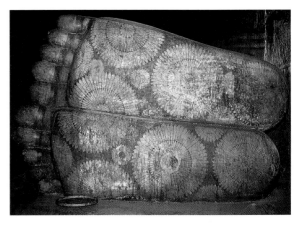

Footwork *The feet of a Buddha in the Dambulla temple in Sri Lanka have been painted with lotus flowers.*

Siddhartha Gautama (*c.*563–*c.*483 BC), the Buddha or 'Enlightened One', came from a Hindu family, from the princely Kshatriya caste. Like others of his time, his first concern was to reform Hinduism, and he focused his criticism on the power and privileges of the Brahman priests, the caste system, the worship of idols and the practice of animal sacrifice. He sought a society that was more just, more egalitarian and non-violent. By example, he demonstrated that the path to Enlightenment lay in meditation and the suppression of desire, and in the pursuit of the 'middle way' through moderation, rather than extreme self-denial. Buddhism teaches that we go through a series of rebirths before we attain a higher spiritual plane that makes possible the attainment of *nirvana* (the absorption of the self into the infinite). In its pure form, Buddhism is not strictly a religion, since it has no god: rather it is a philosophy and a code of morality.

The two vehicles

Buddhism spread rapidly after it was adopted by Emperor Asoka in 250 BC and it became the state religion. The fact that Buddhism shared many of the characteristics of Hinduism – belief in reincarnation and the law of cause and effect (*karma*); the order of the Universe and the code of 'right behaviour' that goes with it (*dharma*) – eased the path to transition. There was an even greater convergence in the Hindu-Tantric Buddhism that developed in the far north of India and Tibet in the 7th century. For their part, the Hindu Brahmans, in their effort to resist the expansion of Buddhism, set about reforming Hinduism.

There was, however, no clear orthodoxy in early Buddhism: the Buddha left no written record of his teachings. During the Gupta dynasty in the 4th century AD, two main schools of Buddhism began to emerge. Theraveda Buddhism is judged by its followers to have stayed closer to the Buddha's original message. It teaches that the path to enlightenment and *nirvana* is an individual quest, and can be achieved only through an austere, disciplined life, as lived by monks in a monastery.

Mahayana Buddhism ('greater vehicle'), a later development, is more relaxed and populist. It sees the incarnation of the Buddha as one manifestation among many others of a transcendent god. As a result, it permits a far broader pantheon of gods, demons and saints, or Bodhisattvas – those who have attained enlightenment,

Holy site *Buddhist monks in their saffron robes meditate at Bodh Gaya, in Bihar, the place where the Buddha attained enlightenment.*

but sacrificed the opportunity to reach *nirvana* (and thereby become a Buddha) by staying among the living to guide others. In Mahayana Buddhism the salvation of everyone can be achieved through the combined beliefs of the community of Buddhists.

Hinduism reclaims its command

Mahayana Buddhism became one of the main religions of India. For many centuries, the Buddhist universities at Nalanda, Bodh Gaya, Taxila, Sravasti, Amaravati and elsewhere attracted pilgrims and students from all over Asia, as did the great monasteries and

cave temples such as Ajanta and Ellora. But Buddhism never succeeded in supplanting Hinduism among the masses. Furthermore, Buddhism suffered from a weak economic structure. The *sanghas*, or communities of mendicant monks, were forbidden to own material goods of any kind and owed their prosperity entirely to the generosity of princely donors. When donations declined, so did the influence of Buddhism. The Brahmans, meanwhile, accumulated the donations given to them and became extremely wealthy landowners. They began to build ornate temples where the great gods, such as Shiva and Vishnu, were venerated. By about the 6th century AD Hinduism was beginning to regain its prestige. The *coup de grâce* came with the Muslim invaders, who systematically massacred Buddhist monks and destroyed the monasteries.

Today, fewer than 0.01 per cent of the Indian population is Buddhist. Theravada Buddhism survived in Sri Lanka, where 65 per cent are Buddhist and the temples and communities of ordained monks (*bhikkhus*) continue to prosper. But in Nepal, the birthplace of the Buddha, the figure is less than 10 per cent.

Objects of veneration *Buddhist monks stand in prayer at Polonnaruwa in Sri Lanka, a former capital in the 8th to 13th centuries. These statues were sculpted from the granite rock: the reclining Buddha is 46 ft (14 m) long, while the standing Buddha is 23 ft (7 m) high.*

Would-be Buddha
This fine 8th- or 9th-century gilt-bronze statue from Sri Lanka shows a Bodhisattva (possibly Avalokitesvara) in the attitude of 'royal ease'.

Images of the Buddha

The Buddha forbade his disciples to make him the object of cult worship after his death, and for many centuries no image of the Buddha appeared in human form: instead, he was represented by symbols. But Hinduism's fascination for images proved irresistible and a tradition of representation began to appear in the 2nd century AD. The Buddha was portrayed with identifying characteristics, a language of hand positions (*mudras*), and poses representing his various attitudes – seated, teaching, fasting, satiated, reclining.

The Jains, protectors of life

Although founded at about the same time, Jainism did not spread like Buddhism, but has followed a more steady trajectory. Today, there are about 4 million Jains in India. Their puritanism and benevolence have earned the respect of all the religious communities, including the Hindus.

Splashes of colour *During the Mahamastakabhishekha festival, held every 12 years, pilgrims pour milk, curd, rice, coconut water, honey and countless other offerings over the 1000-year-old statue of the warrior-prince Bahubali (the first Jain saint), at Sravanabelagola in Karnataka.*

Those who observe scrupulously the 'five vows' of Jainism will not move without taking the precaution of sweeping the ground before each step, and they breathe with the mouth covered with white gauze. For one of the key vows stipulates that all members of the Jain religion must do no harm to any living creature. Even the smallest insect must be protected from the risk of being trodden on or inhaled.

Compassion and respect for all living things

To the Jains, all life is sacred. As every living being is a reincarnation, it has the right to compassion and respect. The supreme virtue is *ahimsa*, 'not to injure or harm'. As with human beings, animals have five senses. They also have *jiva*, the vital principle or soul which allows them to remember their previous lives. When they suffer, it is the duty of humans to care for them. Hence Jains run hospitals for sick animals. Jains are not only strictly vegetarian, but they also abstain from eating certain fruits and roots, for plants also have *jiva*. They do not eat potatoes or onions, as these are thought to harbour micro-organisms.

Most of India's 4 million Jains live in Rajasthan, Gujarat and in southern India. Like Buddhism, with which it has much in common, Jainism developed out of an effort to reform Hinduism, in the 6th century BC. The founder Vardhamana, nicknamed Mahavira (the Great Hero), was born in Bihar in 599 BC. For 12 years he lived as an ascetic, then, having attained enlightenment, he travelled and preached for 30 years, dying at the age of 72.

The 'five vows' are: do no harm to living creatures; always speak the truth; do not steal; be chaste; do not become attached to material possessions. For lay people, lesser vows of non-violence, truthfulness and charity suffice in this life. The ultimate goal is the 'conquest' of enlightenment (the word Jain comes from *Jinas* ('Conquerors'), but this is only really achievable by those leading a monastic life.

There are two orders of Jain monks. The Shvetambaras ('white clothed') dress in white robes; they include nuns. The Digambaras ('sky-clothed') go about naked in their precincts, equipped only with a water gourd and a peacock feather to sweep aside insects without causing them harm. No women are admitted to this order.

Infinite respect *A Jain woman prays with her beads. The soft brooms are used to brush away insects, to prevent them being crushed by footsteps.*

Parsees: keepers of the fire

The Parsees number fewer than 200 000 and so are numerically insignificant amongst the vast statistics of the subcontinent's other religions. But they represent one of the most Westernised groups and play a disproportionately large role in the economy of India.

The Parsees (or Parsis) arrived on the west coast of India in the 8th century AD as refugees fleeing persecution by the Muslims in Persia (Iran). They are among the last survivors of Zoroastrianism, which takes its name from its founder Zoroaster (or Zarathustra), who lived in the 7th century BC. For over 1000 years, from about 559 BC to 651 AD, Zoroastrianism was the state religion of the Achaemenians, the Parthians and the Sasanians in the area now occupied by Iraq, Iran and Afghanistan.

The temple of the sacred flame

The central concept of Zoroastrianism is the opposition of good and evil, a struggle in which good will ultimately triumph. Ahura Mazda is the supreme and only god, who created the world in order to defeat his enemy, Angra Mainyu, the force of evil. One of the first monotheistic religions, Zoroastrianism is thought to have played an influential role in the evolution of Judaism, Christianity and Islam. Fire holds a central place in the cult. The symbol of truth and righteousness, it is the centrepiece of any Parsee place of worship (or 'fire temple'). Flames are kept alight in a bronze vase in an inner sanctuary, where the most sacred rituals are conducted by priests. Zoroastrians pray five times a day, either before a flame at a temple, or facing a source of light at home. As they do so,

Bonds of marriage *Rings are exchanged during the Parsee wedding ceremony.*

they tie and untie a sacred cord (*kusti*) around their waist. The life of a Parsee is punctuated with rituals, from the fifth month of pregnancy until death. Marriage is obligatory, to perpetuate the Parsee community. Parsees are respected by the Hindus, who see them as a kind of caste.

Because the Parsees place comparatively few restrictions on behaviour, they have become one of the most Westernised of all Indian communities. They have been involved in business and manufacture for many centuries, and by the 19th century they had a monopoly of business in Mumbai (Bombay).

City-dwellers *More than 50 per cent of Parsees live in Mumbai.*

The towers of silence

In contrast to other religions of the subcontinent, Parsees are neither buried nor cremated: they believe the sacred elements of earth, fire and water should not be contaminated by death. Instead, corpses are washed, wrapped in a shroud, and taken in an iron coffin to the Towers of Silence (*dakhmas*), where they are devoured by vultures. Accessible only to non-Parsee undertakers, these cylindrical buildings are open to the skies. Inside, a shaft is surrounded by circular balconies on which the bodies are laid, with the face turned to the sky. Once the work of the vultures is done, the bones are thrown down the shaft. According to Parsee beliefs, if the deeds of the dead during their lifetime were good, the soul heads southwards to the Parsee heaven; if they were bad, the soul, stinking and ugly, will head north and into the darkness of hell.

Symbol of faith *Parsee priests tie a sacred cord (*kusti*) around the waists of children at the age of seven. They will wear the cord for the rest of their lives.*

Islam in Indian society

Without Partition in 1947, India would have been the most populous nation in Islam. Today, the subcontinent has three Islamic republics: Pakistan, Bangladesh and the Maldives. And, although a minority with only 12 per cent of the total population, India's Muslim community is still the second largest in the world (after Indonesia).

Path of devotion *Sufis, a mystical and minority sect of Islam, make a pilgrimage in Pakistan. Sufism reached the subcontinent in the 11th century.*

Arab merchants introduced Islam to the southern coasts of India, and made their converts using persuasion and example. But in the north, Islam arrived on the point of the sword, when Turkish Ghaznavids invaded during the 11th century and Qutb-ud-Din Aybak formed the Sultanate of Delhi in the 12th century. Widespread massacres and the destruction of temples continued as the Muslim armies spread eastwards into Bihar and Bengal.

The Koran among the castes

Islam reached its zenith in India under the Mughal emperors, from the reign of the tolerant Akbar to the fanatical Aurangzeb, a period lasting from 1556 to 1707. To many people within Hindu society, especially the low-caste and the Untouchables, Islam had an obvious appeal. It was in principle casteless, and had the attractive simplicity of monotheism. But the higher castes and devout Hindus were caught in a dilemma: rejecting Islam was dangerous, but by adapting they could survive and await a revival of their own traditions. At the same time, Islamic ideology also adapted to the manners and customs of the Hindus. Hence new converts, having abandoned their gods and the worship of idols,

By the book *Pakistani children attending Koranic school in Lahore.*

nonetheless clung to the social hierarchy of a caste system, despite the insistence of the Prophet that all people are equal.

Partition has polarised religious faiths in the subcontinent. Today, 97 per cent of Pakistanis and 87 per cent of Bangladeshis are Muslim. The division between Muslim and Hindu has fuelled extremism among both communities. In Pakistan, fanatical Islamists have backed Al-Qaeda terrorists in Afghanistan and massacred Christians in their churches. Meanwhile, Hindus in India have been responsible for massacres of Muslims in co-ordinated attacks that bear the hallmarks of ethnic cleansing. Despite a history stretching back over 1000 years, Muslims in India today feel threatened and poorly protected.

Conflict *Hindu activists destroyed the mosque at Ayodhya in 1992.*

The battle for Ayodhya

In no place in India is the clash between Hinduism and Islam more acute than in the city of Ayodhya, in Gujarat. In the early 16th century Babur, the first Mughal emperor, had a mosque built on the supposed birthplace of Rama. In 1992 Hindu activists pulled it down, triggering a wave of intercommunal riots in which 2000 people died. Hindu militants are still pressing to build a temple to Rama on the site.

The Sikhs: the 'lions' of India

Sikh means 'disciple' – originally disciples of Guru Nanak, a 16th-century mystic who preached a new approach in answer to the ongoing conflict between Hinduism and Islam. The religion he created combines elements of both.

Born a Hindu of high caste, Guru Nanak (1469-1539) took up work initially in the service of the Sultanate of Delhi, but he abandoned his family and job to seek religious inspiration. Through divine revelation, he learnt that the godhead is a single force, present everywhere, and transcends all religion. Nanak taught that human salvation could be achieved through faith in divine harmony, to which one must be attuned. He placed emphasis on three actions: meditation (usually on God's name, or through chanting hymns); acts of charity; and honest hard work (as opposed to the ascetic practices of monks). Like the Hindus, Sikhs hold that the soul is reborn after death, but that it can be liberated from rebirth by god's grace. Sikhism is monotheistic, and because God is beyond description, he cannot become an idol or be reduced to an image (as in Hinduism).

Nanak preached universal tolerance. He took issue with the Brahmans' obsession with caste and showed compassion towards the Untouchables. By way of example, he invited Hindus of all castes and Muslims to his house to sing praises to God and to share meals – all of which ran contrary to the traditions of Brahmanism.

Focal shrine *Decked in gold leaf, the Golden Temple at Amritsar, in the Indian state of Punjab, is the Sikhs' most sacred temple. It houses the original* **Adi Granth,** *the Sikh holy book.*

Sacred word *The* **Adi Granth** *is the sole object of devotion found within a Sikh* **gurdwara,** *or place of worship. Revered like a living teacher, the book is also known as* **Guru Granth Sahib.**

Today, although just 2 per cent of the population of India, Sikhs number some 20 million. The majority live in the state of Punjab, a farming region that produces a quarter of the nation's grain. But they are also represented in all aspects of city life – politics, the arts, trade, business, transport, the police and the military.

Lions and princesses *Guru Gobind Singh bestowed the name Singh, or 'lion', on male followers to create a sense of cohesion and to throw off the vestiges of caste. Women take the name Kaur ('Princess').*

Sikh terrorism and the assassination of Indira Gandhi

After Partition, Sikhs lobbied for a division of the Indian state of Punjab to provide a homeland for themselves. In 1966 the Hindu-dominated state of Haryana was created, leaving Punjab as a Sikh-dominated state. Militant fundamentalists pushed for an independent Sikh state, Khalistan. In 1978 a splinter group initiated a campaign of violence and terrorism, which induced the Indian government to impose direct rule. In 1982 moderates took up the cause in a series of demonstrations, and Pakistan entered the fray by training militants. On June 2, 1984, Prime Minister Indira Gandhi launched a military assault on the Golden Temple at Amritsar, which had become the headquarters for Sikh terrorists. Nearly 500 were killed, including their leader Jarnail Singh Bhindranwale. In October 1984 Gandhi was assassinated by her Sikh bodyguards, provoking widespread inter-ethnic reprisals across India. Separatist violence continued in Punjab and in 1987 the Indian government declared a state of emergency, but it diminished after concerted police action and elections in 1992.

Nanak was the first in a succession of ten Sikh gurus, the last of whom died in 1708. The last of the gurus, Gobind Singh, created the militaristic institution called the *Khalsa* ('pure') for Sikh males, who bear the 'five Ks', or distinctive Sikh attributes, each of which begin with the letter 'k' in Punjabi: bangle, comb, shorts, sword and uncut hair. The tradition of uncut hair explains why Sikh men wear turbans.

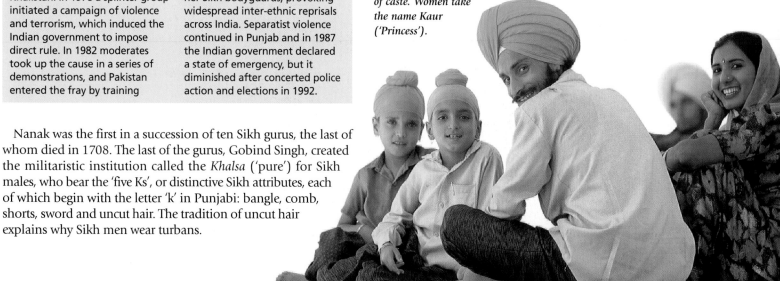

A mosaic of tribes

India has about 400 tribes, representing some 70 million people in all. Often dispossessed of their ancestral lands and threatened by the loss of their traditions, many have spent the past few decades fighting for self-determination.

Bird's-eye view *The Garo people of Meghalaya build watchtowers to keep an eye on wild animals that might enter their lands and damage their crops.*

The tribes of India are collectively called *Adivasi* 'inhabitants since the beginning'. Pushed back into the forests and mountains by waves of invaders, for many centuries they managed to preserve total independence by virtue of their sheer inaccessibility. These days, their distinct cultures and sense of autonomy are being eroded by the drive towards integration – which often looks suspiciously like colonialism under a different name.

On the road to integration

More than half of these so-called 'scheduled tribes' live in central India: about 20 per cent live in Rajasthan, Gujarat and Maharashtra, a further 20 per cent in the north-eastern borderlands of Burma and China, and 6 per cent in southern India.

The Constitution of India provided for a quota system and special concessions for the scheduled tribes, but these have been largely ignored. Meanwhile, the expansion of infrastructure (roads, railways and dams) and the spread of agricultural land has reduced the areas used traditionally for hunting, gathering and fishing, particularly in the Deccan. It has also increased exposure to more mainstream cultures through contact with migrant workers.

Historically, when dispossessed of their lands, or reduced to a position of powerlessness within them, these tribes have resorted to rebellion. The first big revolt was that of the Santals (now in Bangladesh), who marched on Calcutta in 1855. In the 1920s, the Bhils of Rajasthan tried to create an independent kingdom. More recently, the spotlight has been on the Tibeto-Burman peoples living in the heavily forested north-east of India, who have been waging campaigns of armed struggle in and around Assam.

The struggle for self-determination

In the days of the British Raj, the tribal lands on the northern rim of India escaped the full impact of colonisation because they served as a valuable buffer zone, protecting the Empire from aggressors.

Colour sense *Tharu women dress in bright-coloured printed cottons and copious jewellery. Some 800 000 Tharus live in remote areas of the Tarai lowlands in Nepal.*

Entry into the strategic zone on the border with China was restricted to the military and Christian missionaries. At independence, these non-Indian peoples could not easily accept integration into the Indian Union. The Naga tribes (Angami, Ao, Sema, Konyak, Chakesang) to the east of Assam demanded autonomy; some insisted on full independence. In 1952 an insurrection broke out, with an additional frisson supplied by the Nagas' fearsome reputation as head-hunters. During the 1960s, the rebellion received the support of communist China, under Mao Tse-tung, and it spread to the neighbouring Mizo (or Lushai). The Khasi, Garo and Jaintia of the Shillong plateau then joined arms in a struggle for their own state, Meghalaya ('Abode of the Clouds').

As a result of political pressure and guerrilla activity over a period of some 20 years, a new set of states emerged to the south and east of Assam. Nagaland became a self-governing state in 1963; however, insurrection and sabotage has continued, despite a cease-fire in 1975. Meghalaya became a state in 1972. Armed rebellion was waged by the Mizo National Front until the state of Mizoram ('Land of the Highlanders') was created in 1987.

Tribes, most of them Buddhist and speaking more than 50 different languages among them, live among the forests and mountains of Arunachal Pradesh. This borderland region in the far north-east of India is also claimed by China, which attempted to invade in 1959-62. It became a state in 1986. The state of Manipur, on the border with Burma, was created in 1972. Its population is composed of more than 30 tribes, including the Nagas and the Meithei ethnic group, which represents 60 per cent of the total. The Meitheis have a warrior tradition and excel in the martial arts, in javelin-throwing and sword-fighting. They also play polo, and some credit them with inventing the game. The state of Tripura, bordering Bangladesh, was also formed in 1972, but the central government imposed direct rule in 1993 in the face of tribal insurrection. This is home to the Kuki, Chakma and Mogh, who number also among the 20 tribal groups found in Bangladesh, along with the Marma, Rakhaine, Murang, Santal, Malpahari, Khasi and Garo.

Integration, and the exceptions

Most tribes in India have accepted integration and shed their warlike traditions. Originally animist, many described themselves as Hindu at the most recent census; others are Christian. In the northeastern states, tribal peoples live by slash and burn agriculture. This also applies to many groups in the south, although the Todas of Tamil Nadu depend largely on their buffalo for food, and the Malapantaram of Kerala are semi-nomadic hunter-gatherers. In Pakistan, the Muslim tribal peoples living in the harsh lands of the North-West Frontier Province have managed to preserve their autonomy.

Self-expression For the Naga peoples of Assam, dance is a way of expressing their distinctive culture.

The Todas

There are some 2000 Todas living in about six villages in the Nilgiri Hills of Tamil Nadu, near Ootacamund. They wear a robe called a *put-kuli*, made of thick cotton with decorative stripes of white, red, blue and black. Their economy, indeed their whole culture, centres upon the water buffalo and the milk it provides. Only men have access to their temples, where they pay homage to Tekirishi, the goddess who created the buffalo. Here the priest churns the milk of a sacred buffalo. The Toda marry very young, for no one must die unmarried. Children have a natural father as well as a social father, through whom they acquire rank in the tribal hierarchy. Efforts have been made to revive Toda culture, which has been threatened with extinction in recent years.

Dress code Men and women of the Toda wear striped robes.

Same, but different Adi women sort rice, which is a familiar activity all over India. The Adi live in the thickly forested regions of Arunachal Pradesh.

A profusion of dialects and languages

India has 18 major languages and more than 150 other languages, a great many of which are spoken by several million people. Language is, of course, closely tied to ethnicity, and so can become a burning issue – literally.

Single currency *India's multilingual character is self-evident from its banknotes for the national currency, the rupee.*

The diversity of languages in India is recognised and upheld by the Constitution: 'Any section of the citizens residing in the territory of India or any part thereof having a distinct language, script or culture of its own shall have the right to conserve the same.' (Article 29). But some languages are more equal than others.

The national language issue

After independence, India wanted to choose a national language. Dravidians in the south fiercely resisted what they saw as the linguistic imperialism of the north (and of Hindi). In 1950, as a compromise, English was chosen as an official language for a period of 15 years. During this time the use of Hindi was cultivated as the potential national language and was a compulsory subject in schools. When the question came up for review in 1965, the Dravidian states still opposed the adoption of Hindi as a national language, and so after more than 50 years English remains an official language and is still the lingua franca of the elite.

Indic and Dravidian

Hindi is spoken by more than a third of the population, primarily in the north and north-west. It has two main forms, Western Hindi and Eastern Hindi, and many dialect variations. It belongs to the Indic, or Indo-Aryan, group of languages, which accounts for 73 per cent of the languages of India and includes Bengali, Urdu, Marathi, Gujarati, Punjabi, Oriya, Assamese, Kashmiri, Sindhi and Nepali. Sanskrit, a written language essential for reading sacred texts, also belongs to this group. These are some of the 18 state languages that can be used in schools and administration. Bihari, an Indic language of north-eastern India, is a notable exception from this list, even though it is spoken by 40 million people.

News-stand *Pakistani readers catch up with the news from papers hung out in the street. The official language is Urdu, but Punjabi, Pashto, Saraiki, Baluchi and English are spoken, along with many others.*

The languages
- Indo-European
  - Hindi
  - Bengali
- Dravidian
- Tibeto-Burman
- Munda
- Mon-Khmer

Good read *Children in Ladakh are among the 200 million young Indians who can benefit from free, compulsory schooling to the age of 14.*

Most of the other state languages belong to the Dravidian group, spoken mainly in the south of India by 24 per cent of the population: Tamil (also spoken in parts of Sri Lanka), Malayalam, Telugu and Kannada (Kanarese). The Dravidian languages have ancient origins and were spoken across the subcontinent at the time of Mohenjo-Daro, before the Aryan invasions 3500 years ago. Manipuri is the only state language from the Tibeto-Burman group.

In a group of their own are the Munda languages, also vestiges of pre-Aryan times, and now spoken only in north-east and central India. Santali is the most widespread of these. They are believed to be related to the South-east Asian group, which include the Mon-Khmer languages, such as Khasi, spoken in Assam and Meghalaya.

Urdu: born of invasion

The official language of Pakistan is Urdu, but only about 10 per cent of the Pakistani population speaks it as a first language. It is closely related to Hindi, but has an Islamic orientation, with elements from Persian and Arabic. It is also spoken by the Muslims in India. The other languages common to India and Pakistan are Punjabi and Sindhi.

Writ large   Nepalese is the main language of Sikkim (right), where nearly 70 per cent of the population is of Nepalese origin.

Language plays a significant role in Pakistan's national politics because the country is divided into provinces along language lines. Each enjoys a certain amount of autonomy and has its own regional assembly. In Baluchistan, Brahui is spoken by an ethnic minority, who represent a vestige of the Dravidian-speakers of pre-Aryan times. In the former princely states of the North-West Frontier, mountain peoples speak dialects that have no written form and which have no known connection with any linguistic family.

Nepali, derived from Sanskrit, serves as the lingua franca in Nepal – but it is the mother tongue of only slightly more than half the population. Nepal has 35 or so other languages, which have managed to preserve their integrity in the isolation of high mountain valleys.

In Sri Lanka, three-quarters of the population are Sinhalese – most of them Buddhists – who speak Sinhala. The mainly Hindu north is Tamil-speaking. The official language of the Maldives is Divehi, another Indic language.

Words of wisdom   A school sign in Mahabalipuram, in Tamil Nadu, is written in Tamil, a Dravidian language with a rich tradition.

The flavours of Indian cookery

Is there a city in Europe that does not have at least one restaurant serving Indian or Pakistani food? Yet, despite this exposure, real Indian cooking remains little understood outside the subcontinent. The rich, heavily spiced, chilli-hot food with which it is casually associated abroad plays only a small part in the story.

Aid to digestion   *After a meal, many Indians chew on a wad of* pan. *This comprises betelnut mixed with various spices and a paste made of the mineral lime and sometimes tobacco, all wrapped in an edible leaf. Chewing stimulates saliva, which is ejected as a jet of red spittle.*

To the vast majority living in the Indian subcontinent, food is very simple. It consists of the staple – rice or wheat – plus *dal* (a purée of pulses, such as lentils) and some kind of relish, chutney or yoghurt condiment. On occasions a meat or fish dish might be included, and just about every version of this formula will have some kind of spices added. Thereafter, any uniformity of cuisine evaporates. Every region has its own special flavours, its own

Spice world   *A street trader in Delhi sells spices and dry foods from his pavement store, filling the air with a spice-laden scent.*

favourite dishes with which it is associated; from the hearty mutton stews of Kashmir, such as *rogan josh*, to the fiery prawn dishes and rice pancakes of Kerala. The Indian cookery of the Western world is largely Punjabi in origin, brought by émigrés from that troubled region after Partition; in their traditional charcoal-burning *tandoor* ovens they produced such well-known dishes as chicken *tandoori* and *tikka*, with their distinctive red colouring.

The spice of life

Even the staples vary from region to region. Rice is the staple of southern, eastern and western India, but there are many kinds of rice and ways to cook it. In Assam it is sticky; in the south it is made into rice cakes, called *idlis*. The much-cherished basmati (literally, 'aromatic') rice comes from the foothills of the Himalayas. Wheat is the staple of the north, where it is eaten as bread (*roti*) in its many forms: cooked plain on a griddle (*chapati*), deep-fried (*puris*), shallow-fried (*parathas*), or baked in an oven (*naan*).

Regional dishes are an expression of the geography, climate, history and religion of the area. Pork and beef appear rarely, as they

Tea break   *Itinerant tea-vendors take a rest in a park in Calcutta. A vestige of the British Raj, sweetened milky tea is the national drink.*

The myth of curry

There is no such thing as curry powder in India, except in the warehouses of Kerala, where spices are ground to a formula for the export market. It is alien to Indian cookery, where every dish demands its own carefully balanced flavourings and the delicate judgment of the cook. The only equivalent of curry powder in an Indian kitchen is the mixture of ground spices called garam masala, used as a garnish for food nearing the end of the cooking process. Containing cardamom seeds, cinnamon, black cumin, cloves, black peppercorns and nutmeg, it has a far more delicate, scented flavour than curry powder, which usually also contains turmeric, coriander, fenugreek and red chilli. The word curry appears to derive from the Tamil *kari*, meaning sauce. It was adopted by the British to refer to any spiced Indian dish, and spice exporters devised a recipe for curry powder that would help them recall the flavours of India when they returned home.

are taboo among Muslims and Hindus. The most commonly eaten meats are chicken, lamb and goat. The *mughlai* or Mughal dishes of the north, fragrant with almonds and dried fruit, reflect the Persian cooking imported by the Mughal emperors. The most famous dish of Orissa is *ghanto tarkari*, a combination of root crops such as yam, potatoes and taro leaves mixed with cauliflower, peas and coconut. Asafetida, a plant resin with a pungent onion-like smell, is widely used throughout India to flavour curries, meatballs and pickles.

A meal may end with some sliced fruits, which express more than any other food the huge variety of climate across the subcontinent. While Kashmir produces apples and strawberries, the south has the full range of tropical fruits, such as bananas, guava and papaya.

The basic ingredients *Across India, kitchens often consist of little more than a clay oven and an open fire.*

Snacks and sweets

Indians tend to eat often. The two main meals, taken at midday and in the evening, are interspersed with snacks, often supplied by a street vendor – such as a pasty-like *samosa*, or a deep-fried vegetable fritter (*bhaji*). They also love sweets, which are associated particularly with festivals. These include numerous concoctions made of reduced (evaporated) milk, such as the brightly-coloured, fudge-like *barfi* and *gulab jamums* – soft, spongy egg-shaped balls of deep-fried dough made with reduced milk, doused in sugar syrup and flavoured with rosewater. Milk products contribute to Indian food in a number of ways: yoghurt-based condiments such as *raita*, served with the main meal; as the cheese *paneer*, used in both savoury dishes and sweets; as reduced milk in sweets and the rich, chewy ice cream called *kulfi*; and as ghee, the much-prized clarified butter used widely as a cooking fat. Yoghurt is used to make the refreshing drink *lassi*, which may be served either salty or sweet. Fresh juices are made of lime, sugar cane, pineapple, guava and other fruits – but fizzy drinks and colas are also popular.

Freshly fried *A doughnut seller prepares his wares at the Sonepur fair, in Bihar.*

Home life *Tea is served in a home in Gujarat. It is common practice to eat seated on the ground, rather than around a table.*

87

The art of dressing

Across the subcontinent, each region and ethnic group still clings to its traditions of dress. These evolved over hundreds of years, providing garments that are perfectly adapted to the climate. Nonetheless, the influence of international styles is proving irresistible, and everyday clothes are becoming increasingly standardised, particularly among the young.

There was once a time when the subcontinent was dressed by craft-based fabric-makers and tailors. While maharajas and their wives inspired legends with their exquisitely tailored silk brocades and copious jewels, ordinary people were comfortable in their loose-fitting cotton clothes, spun and woven at home, in the manner that Gandhi attempted to promote. But changing patterns of behaviour and the development of the textile industries have squeezed out the artisans and many traditional styles of dress.

Suit, sari and turban

The lounge suit, or a shirt and tie, is the uniform of businessmen, office workers and professionals. But at home, men tend to put on the traditional cotton clothes of the man-in-the-street: a long shirt (*kurta*) worn over baggy trousers (*pyjama*). The *dhoti* is a long piece of white cloth hung from the waist and drawn up between the legs. The equivalent in the south is a *lungi*, a length of printed cloth worn like a sarong. A waistcoat or jacket with a straight collar completes the outfit. A low-caste man, often seen bare-chested in the countryside, may wear a *langoti*, a kind of loincloth.

The Sikhs are just about the only men who wear turbans in the city, but turbans are more common in the countryside, among Muslims as well as Hindus. The piece of cloth used may be 30 ft (9 m) long. The Nepalese wear a small, rimless hat, while Kashmiris prefer a beret-like cap made of astrakhan lamb's wool.

The most common form of women's clothing is the sari, which consists of a single piece of cloth 16–30 ft (5–9 m) long and 3 ft (1 m) wide. It may be made of cotton, silk or synthetic fabric. Saris are worn with a *choli*, a small, tightly-fitting blouse that reaches down to beneath the breasts. The cloth is wrapped, tucked and pleated over the *pavada*, a long petticoat, and the remaining length, the *palloo*, is thrown over the left shoulder.

At ease *The traditional form of clothing for men in Pakistan is similar to the* **kurta-pyjama** *of India, but here it is called the* **shalwar kameez.**

Sari style *There are more than 100 different ways to wear a sari, which vary according to region, caste and personal preference.*

Western medicine versus ancient traditions of healthcare

The days of great famines and frequent epidemics now appear to be over and life-expectancy in the Indian subcontinent has risen rapidly. Western medicine has come to the subcontinent's aid, but ancient systems of ayurvedic medicine still endure and may provide a vital resource for future remedies.

Pharmacy *Ayurvedic medicines in Thekkady, Kerala.*

In India, Pakistan and Sri Lanka, life expectancy has more than doubled over the past 75 years. In the 1930s, the average age at death was a mere 27. Food shortages may still occur, but the great famines are a thing of the past. Thanks to vaccines, epidemics of cholera and typhoid no longer wreak such havoc, and smallpox has been eradicated. Nonetheless, other problems have come to the fore: malaria, which was once in retreat, is now on the increase again, due to insecticide- and drug-resistant strains of the mosquito and the parasite it carries. Tuberculosis and leprosy are still the scourge of the poor. Diseases carried by water-borne parasites are also common. And AIDS, transmitted mainly through prostitution, has now affected an estimated 10 million people.

Recycling *A specialist in dental products presents his wares in Calcutta.*

Science for a long life

Before Western medicine reached the subcontinent, the principal system of treatment was ayurvedic. Ayurveda is the *veda* (science or knowledge) of the *ayus* (life, vitality, health and longevity). Originating in ancient times and codified in the sacred *Veda* texts, it began as a mixture of magic and herbal medicine. But Indian medicine became scientific at an early stage and doctors learnt from the Greeks and the Persians, leaders in the field in their day.

Ayurvedic medicine built up knowledge about the efficacy of some 2000 plants, and more than 500 of these are still widely used today. Because Brahmans forbade dissection and all contact with blood, ayurvedic doctors knew very little about anatomy until the 19th century. Nonetheless, even in ancient times, surgery was performed, including cataract operations, the removal of gallstones, caesareans and even skin grafts. But surgery was considered a last resort: most treatment was administered through plant- or mineral-based medicines and additional therapies such as fumigation, baths and massage. Ayurvedic medicine was above all preventative: the aim was to keep the three humours, bile, phlegm and wind, in tune with the primary bodily elements – blood, flesh, fat, bone, marrow, sperm. Rigorous hygiene was considered essential.

As the search for new cures continues, ayurvedic and other traditional forms of Indian medicine are being mined for their knowledge. Some of India's medicinal plants, such as the neem tree, are now being investigated by international pharmaceutical companies, and may even hold the key to a cure for AIDS.

The dangers of water

Hindus believe that water is the source of purification, and a sacred river like the Ganges is said to be free of all germs when it passes through Varanasi (Benares). But water is a carrier of diseases such as typhoid, cholera, dysentery and hepatitis. Many towns have no drainage systems and 20 per cent of the population have no access to clean water. Providing more clean water and better sanitation is a major priority of the Indian central government.

Morning ritual *Men clean their teeth by the Hugli River in Calcutta.*

A passion for sport and games

Several of the sports played on the Indian subcontinent, including polo, archery and kalaripayattu, have a local history stretching back thousands of years. But their role in society has been largely usurped by sports introduced by the British, such as tennis, golf, squash, soccer and cricket – the great national sport of India, Pakistan and Sri Lanka. As elsewhere in the world, television has played a major role in accelerating this conversion.

Targeting success   *Archery is the national sport of Bhutan, where tournaments are held in a carnival atmosphere.*

In the days of the maharajas, public festivals included elephant combat and camel races. Today bull combat still takes place in the Punjab, and quails and partridges are made to fight in the bazaars of Pakistan, and are the subject of massive and illicit gambling. In Baluchistan, flocks of pigeons are released in a popular game: the aim is to attract the flock of the opponent and capture it in a net; the loser then has to pay to retrieve his flock.

Various countries claim to have invented hockey: a version was played in the Hunza Valley, in northern Pakistani Kashmir, before the modern game evolved. It is still played with great skill and

Highland game   *Several countries claim to have invented polo, including Pakistan (shown here), Tibet, Iran and Mongolia, where a similar game was played with a goat carcass.*

enthusiasm: India and Pakistan dominated Olympic field hockey from 1928-84, but have been edged out of the medals since then. The ancestry of polo is similarly disputed. It was a popular sport at the imperial court of the Mughals before it was taken up by the British, who codified the rules to produce the modern game. Like hunting and golf, it remains a sport of the elite.

Archery is the greatest sporting passion in Bhutan. Skills are tested over a distance of 160 yd (145 m), traditionally using a bamboo arrow, strung with plant fibres and arrows flighted with pheasant or eagle feathers that have fallen naturally (since killing animals is taboo in Bhutan). Archery is the only sport for which Bhutan enters a team at the Olympics, but it has yet to win a medal, although its archers have been rewarded with some success in other international games.

Warm-up Young cricketers limber up on a pitch in Bombay. Cricket pitches often provide a calm oasis of green amid the heat and dust of the subcontinent.

Squash and cricket

Other games have been unquestionably imported. For many years after independence, Pakistan was the undisputed world master of the game of squash. Jahangir Khan was the world's leading player throughout the 1980s. Then, in 1993, he was eclipsed by his near namesake, Jansher Khan – not in fact a relative, but from the same village of Nawakille, near Peshawar – who went on to win a record eight world championships.

Cricket incites the greatest passions. The top players are major celebrities and receive adulation that borders on fanaticism.

During international matches, people follow the commentary with transistor radios pressed to their ears. Each nation has its heroes, such as Sachin Tendulkar and Sourav Ganguly of India; and Wasim Akram and Waqar Younis of Pakistan. Most of the top players also play abroad, mainly for English teams. In recent years both Pakistan and India have been accused of match-fixing and ball-tampering – a measure perhaps of the passions that professional cricket incites.

Kalaripayattu: the original martial art

The traditional discipline of combat called kalaripayattu may well be the ancestor of other martial arts. Developed in the Indian subcontinent, it is said to have been introduced to East Asia in the 6th century by the semi-legendary monk Bodhidharma, father of Zen Buddhism. He went to China and founded a monastery at Shaolin and taught the monks kalaripayattu as a means of defence against bandits. It later spread to Japan, the homeland of many martial arts.

Kalaripayattu, 'the way of the battlefield', is described in palm-leaf manuscripts dating from the 2nd century BC, and is still taught in the state of Kerala in southern India. More a way of life than a sport, especially for the local

Hindu warrior caste, it takes 10 years or more to learn. Pupils, both male and female, can start training from the age of seven, taking instruction from a guru, or master. Training sessions begin with oiling and massaging the body, followed by a series of warm-up routines. Combatants start by using the *silambam*, a stick made of very hard wood, then move on to metal swords and long batons. The *otta* is a kind of spear made of wood or horn in the shape of an elephant tusk, while the *urimi* is a highly flexible blade, 6 ft (2 m) long. For defence, combatants have leather shields. Masters of kalaripayattu identify 108 vulnerable points of the body, paralleled with the pressure points of acupuncture.

Masters of their art Kalaripayattu is famous for its spectacular leaps and the dramatic clash of weapons. Contests are fought in a pit called a kalari.

Between democracy and dictatorship

At their independence in 1947-8, India, Pakistan and Sri Lanka acquired the political institutions of parliamentary democracies. Democracy has had a rough ride since, rocked by military coups, political assassinations, martial law, states of emergency, guerrilla wars and intercommunal strife. Despite all the pressures that threaten to push it off course, India remains the world's largest democracy – and is deeply proud of it.

Of all the countries of the subcontinent, Pakistan has had the greatest struggle to make democracy work. In 1977, in one of the most controversial sequences of political upheaval, Prime Minister Zulfikar Ali Bhutto was deposed in a coup by a military junta led by General Zia ul-Haq. Two years later, accused of ordering the assassination of one of his political enemies, Bhutto was hanged.

Islam and democracy

A close ally of Islamic political factions, General Zia governed with a rod of iron and imposed his version of Islamic martial law based on Koranic *sharia* law. Even he, however, sought the legitimacy of the ballot box, and was re-elected as president through a referendum in 1984. Then, in 1988, he died in a mysterious plane crash. Following elections, a fragile democracy seemed about to re-emerge: Benazir, the daughter of Bhutto, became prime minister in December 1988. Less than two years later, she was dismissed for nepotism and corruption. After new elections, the Islamic factions returned in force, but the conservative Prime Minister Nawaz Sharif became embroiled in a struggle for power with the president and was forced out of office in 1993. Benazir Bhutto was then re-elected, but again surrounded herself with corrupt ministers. In 1996 she and her husband were convicted for corruption, but by then Bhutto was living in exile.

Red flags Communists parade in the streets of Calcutta.

In 1997 Nawaz Sharif returned to power, and the *sharia* was adopted as the principal system of law in the country. Two years later Sharif was toppled by General Musharraf, who imposed military rule. Parliamentary elections were held in October 2002 as part of a gradual transition back to democracy.

The world's biggest democracy

Apart from a few brief interludes, the Congress Party held power in India for more than 40 years after independence. Initially, it was led by Jawaharlal Nehru, the architect of independence. Two years after his death in 1964, his daughter Indira Gandhi became prime minister. During the next 11 years of her administration she became increasingly authoritarian, imposing a state of emergency from 1975 to 1977, during which numerous political opponents were

Among friends Benazir Bhutto is acclaimed by supporters as she arrives at Karachi airport.

Armed force Young Tamils train to fight for their independence at a camp in Sri Lanka.

detained, elections were postponed and the press was censored. She was defeated in 1977, but returned to power in 1980 as leader of the new Congress-I Party (I for Indira). During this new period of rule, she used force to quash ethnic disturbances, particularly those caused by separatist movements in Assam and Punjab. Meanwhile,

she encouraged her son Rajiv to enter politics, and in 1981 he was elected to parliament. After his mother's assassination in 1984, he won an overwhelming vote of support as her successor, but, unable to solve the continuing ethnic violence, lost the elections in 1989. His opposition to the Tamils' campaign for independence in Sri Lanka cost him his life: in 1991, while on the campaign trail in southern India, he was the victim of a suicide bomber.

Since the mid 1990s the Congress Party has been eclipsed by other parties, including the increasingly vociferous Hindu nationalists. The Hindu national party, Bharitiya Janata Party (BJP), formed the largest in the 24-party coalition elected to government in 1999, and its leader Atal Behari Vajpayee returned to power as prime minister.

Bangladesh tottered from one military government to the next virtually from its inception, until the elections of 1991 brought Begum Khaleda Zia, widow of the assassinated President Mujibur Rahman, to power as prime minister. She was re-elected in 2001. Sri Lanka has clung on to democracy throughout the civil war waged by the Tamil Tigers against the Sinhalese majority since 1983. An indefinite ceasefire was announced in 2002.

Showing support A wall in Calcutta bears the emblem of the Congress Party – a hand painted in colours of the Indian flag – during the national elections in 1996.

Military dictator General Zia ul-Haq was president of Pakistan from 1978 until his death in 1988.

Prime minister Indira Gandhi inspects a guard of honour in Delhi in 1967, in her second year in office.

Indira, revered and reviled

The daughter of Jawaharlal Nehru, first prime minister of independent India, Indira Gandhi married Feroze Gandhi in 1942 and was unrelated to Mahatma Gandhi. Elected prime minister in 1966, she was a dominant figure in Indian politics for the next 18 years. Many admired her iron will and courage, particularly in facing down separatist violence in the interests of preserving the unity of India. Others never forgave her for the excesses of the state of emergency from 1975 to 1977, or for the sterilisation programme introduced to control population growth.

CHAPTER 4

THE CITIES OF SOUTHERN ASIA

Some of the first cities developed on the Indian subcontinent. Once they were among the most sophisticated and orderly in the world, but now they are more associated with deprivation. In sprawling metropolises across the region families eke out wretched lives in crowded, insanitary slums, or set up their night camps on the city pavements. The squalor is compounded by inadequate drainage and lack of clean water, the constant racket and fumes of dense traffic, buildings in a state of collapse, and public services stretched to breaking point, or non-existent. Much of this is to do with numbers: Mumbai (Bombay), Calcutta, Dhaka, Karachi and Delhi rank among the 15 most populous cities in the world. This obscures the fact that Southern Asia is primarily rural: 75 per cent of the people live in the countryside, but whenever the countryside comes under pressure, it is the cities that take the strain.

The old 'blue city' of Jodhpur, in Rajasthan, fans out from the fort that crowns a rocky ridge.

Mumbai: glamour and misery

Mumbai (Bombay) is India's principal port and the largest city in Southern Asia. It is a microcosm of India, with representatives of all cultures, ethnic origins and religions. But its reputation for mutual respect and tolerance has been rocked by bouts of violence.

Another world *The Gateway of India, inaugurated by the British in 1924, presents an otherworldly backdrop for meditation.*

In the 16th century, the Portuguese recognised the potential of a collection of islands inhabited by Koli fishermen. According to some, they called it *bom bahia*, 'good bay'. Others claim they simply adapted the Koli name, based on their goddess Mumba. The port really only began to develop under the British: the largest island came into their possession when it was included in Catherine of Braganza's dowry on her marriage to Charles II in 1661. The East India Company took a lease on the islands and encouraged settlement by promising religious tolerance. Merchants came from all parts of the subcontinent, and hence Mumbai has communities of Hindus, Muslims, Parsees, Jains, Sikhs, Christians and Jews. Reclamation in the 18th and 19th centuries gradually fused the seven main islands into one, which was connected to the mainland by bridges. Since that time, the city has expanded exponentially: now, with 18.1 million inhabitants, it ranks alongside Mexico City as the second largest city in the world, after Tokyo.

The best and the worst

A population growth of such proportions, on land that is poorly suited to sustain it, has created a serious problem of overcrowding. Mumbai has the world's biggest slums, and in some parts the urban misery is extreme. Three-quarters of the city's inhabitants live in housing deemed inadequate or unsafe, yet there is relatively little unemployment and the people benefit from a generally liberal and tolerant society.

However, this city of all religions is also the heartland of one of the most extremist movements in the land: Shiv Sena, a Hindu nationalist party that lobbies for the local Maratha population. In 1985 the election of its leader stirred up intercommunal tensions. The nationwide turmoil triggered by the destruction by Hindu extremists of the mosque in Ayodhya was particularly acute in Mumbai; in 1992 and 1993 riots and bombings claimed 1200 lives. It was Shiv Sena that encouraged the change in name from Bombay to their Marathi version, Mumbai – and so its usage remains controversial. The process is ongoing, and all the old British names for streets and places in the city are being assigned new Marathi names.

Fresh from the sea *Koli fishermen unload their catches at Sassoon Dock.*

Taking the air *Strolling on Marine Drive.*

Neo-Gothic style   *The Victoria Terminus was built in the late 19th-century.*

Economic muscle

Notwithstanding its troubles, Mumbai has become the wealthiest city in the Indian subcontinent. It is home to 150 banks and the principal stock exchange in the country, and it has the biggest port. It is developing state-of-the-art industries in chemicals and pharmaceuticals, and, most famous of all, is home to the world's most productive cinema industry. Alongside this industrial success, Mumbai has also been able to maintain a flourishing craft and small enterprise sector, composed of hundreds of small companies, which sustain much of the incoming rural workforce. Vast numbers of *wallahs* ply their trades: the *pani-wallahs*, or water-carriers; the *dabba-wallahs*, who deliver cooked meals; the *dhobi-wallahs*, who do the laundry.

Some will claim that this extraordinary development could not have taken place without the protection of the city's patron deity Ganesha, the focus of the great annual Ganesh Chaturthi Festival.

Meals on wheels   *Some 5000 white-capped dabba-wallahs deliver more than 150 000 lunches to offices every day. The meals are prepared each morning, then despatched in insulated containers.*

Others ascribe good fortune to Mahalaxmi, the goddess of wealth and prosperity. A temple to her disappeared centuries before the British decided to build a causeway linking Malabar Hill to Worli Island in the 1890s. The story goes that a Hindu labourer dreamed it would not be achieved until a lost statue of Mahalaxmi was unearthed on the site. This miraculously occurred, a shrine was built to her, and the causeway was duly completed.

Diamonds and the Queen's Necklace

Perhaps Mahalaxmi is also to thank for the prosperity of the diamond district of Mumbai. With a turnover that has more than doubled in the past ten years, Mumbai has become one of the world's leading centres for diamond cutting. Appropriately, the diamond quarter lies close to Marine Drive, the elegant promenade overlooking the Arabian Sea. This has been dubbed the Queen's Necklace because, as night falls, it is lit up by thousands of street lamps that delineate its curving path, creating one of the most memorable seafronts in all Asia.

The caves of Elephanta Island

The Gateway of India is the starting point for excursions to Elephanta Island, also known as Gharapuri, 'place of caves'. This is a top tourist attraction, famed for rock carvings thought to have been created between AD 450 and 750. The 5½ mile (9 km) journey is impressive: the boat weaves among the cargo ships, past numerous small islands used as docks, and past Mumbai's nuclear power plant. On the island itself, it is sadly impossible to see the statue that gave it its Portuguese name. A huge stone sculpture of an elephant collapsed in 1814, at least partly because the Portuguese had used it for target practice – the British re-erected it in Victoria Gardens, where it can still be seen today. The natural caves on the island still contain sculptures of Shiva, including an androgynous Shiva that combines both sexes in a single image, and a three-headed Shiva with the heads representing his three facets as creator, preserver and destroyer.

Multifaceted   *Sculptures of Shiva at Elephanta Island.*

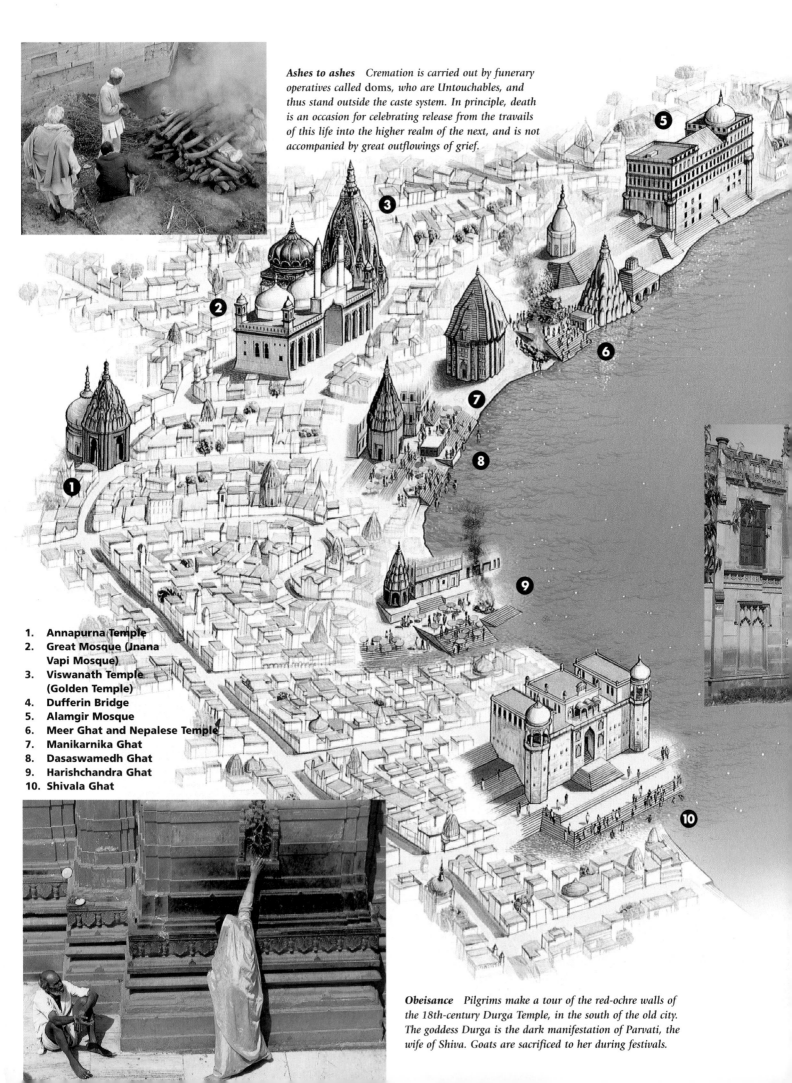

Ashes to ashes *Cremation is carried out by funerary operatives called* doms, *who are Untouchables, and thus stand outside the caste system. In principle, death is an occasion for celebrating release from the travails of this life into the higher realm of the next, and is not accompanied by great outflowings of grief.*

1. **Annapurna Temple**
2. **Great Mosque (Jnana Vapi Mosque)**
3. **Viswanath Temple (Golden Temple)**
4. **Dufferin Bridge**
5. **Alamgir Mosque**
6. **Meer Ghat and Nepalese Temple**
7. **Manikarnika Ghat**
8. **Dasaswamedh Ghat**
9. **Harishchandra Ghat**
10. **Shivala Ghat**

Obeisance *Pilgrims make a tour of the red-ochre walls of the 18th-century Durga Temple, in the south of the old city. The goddess Durga is the dark manifestation of Parvati, the wife of Shiva. Goats are sacrificed to her during festivals.*

Varanasi, holiest of cities

Varanasi (or Benares, as it was known under the British) is the greatest holy city in the subcontinent, venerated by the Hindus, the Jains, and by millions of Buddhists, for it was near here that the Buddha gave his first sermon. Now effectively the religious capital of India, it was founded in about the 7th century BC. The primary focus is the River Ganges, and the west bank is lined with ghats, which face the rising sun. The city once had 1500 temples, but it was destroyed by the Huns in the 6th century and by the Muslims on several occasions – notably under the Mughal Emperor Aurangzeb, who rejected the spirit of tolerance of his forebears. The current population of the city is about 2 million, but every year their numbers are swelled by millions of pilgrims who come here to seek purification in the water of the Ganges, or to die. For this is the holiest place to die, and those who end their lives here can hope to achieve moksha – eternal release from the cycle of life and death.

Pure silk   Silk saris, with gold or silver brocade, are a speciality of Varanasi. Held to be a pure fabric, silk is used to dress statues of the divinities in the temples for religious ceremonies. Because of this tradition, silk-weaving workshops can be found not only in Varanasi, but in all the major pilgrimage centres.

Flames of devotion   Prayers are offered to Ganga, the guardian divinity of the river, on the Tulsi Ghat. An oil-lamp candelabra has been lit to accompany rituals for the annual festival (held in October-November) of Karttikeya – god of war and the planet Mars, and by some accounts the son of Shiva and Ganga.

Twice holy   The Great Mosque dominates the skyline above the ghats. Built in the 17th century by the Mughal Emperor Aurangzeb, it was erected on a site dedicated to Shiva, so it also remains the focus of Hindu devotion. After the destruction of the mosque at Ayodhya by Hindu fanatics, tensions surround this and other Varanasi mosques.

Varanasi

1. Prayers to the gods
A devotee turns in prayer towards the rising sun, during a ritual bath in the Ganges. The river, sacred to both Hindus and Jains, is considered to be the Mother of India, descended from the Heavens. Of all the great pilgrimage centres on the river, including Haridwar and Allahabad, Varanasi is the most sacred. Bathing in its waters is said to wash away all sins. Those whose ashes are scattered in the Ganges can be assured of a better lot in the next life.

2. Travelling around
Because of the narrow streets and the throngs of people, bicycles, rickshaws and pedicabs are the only vehicles permitted in much of the city.

3. Temple steps
Kedar Ghat is one of dozens of stepped river banks (called ghats) that give direct access to the river. These 'Steps of Shiva' – Kedar is one of Shiva's many names – are decorated with lingams (stylised phallic symbols), his emblem. At the top is a temple dedicated to the god by the Bengalis.

4. Burning ghats
A body, shrouded and garlanded, is taken down the Manikarnika Ghat, most sacred of all the ghats, to be cremated. Privileged people may be cremated on the Charanpaduka, a stone slab bearing the footprints of Vishnu. A pool above the steps, called the Manikarnika Well, is said to have been dug by Shiva to recover an earring dropped by his wife Parvati.

5. Road block
Sacred cows bide their time in a street in the middle of the city.

Delhi, the old and the new

The history of Delhi, capital of India, can still be read in the fabric of the modern city. Countless ancient monuments are dotted around the more recent city of New Delhi, which was laid out on a grand imperial scale by the British to the south of Old Delhi. Delhi remains a city with a split personality: Old and New Delhi sometimes act as though the other does not exist.

Pedal power   *Bicycle rickshaws add to the congestion of the streets.*

More than 11 million people live in Delhi, making it the third largest city in India. Once dubbed the 'Rome of Asia', it is a bewildering mix. New Delhi sits astride a vast avenue built on a dehumanising scale, with its grand embassies and government buildings let down by dilapidated concrete monstrosities. The old city is telescoped into a labyrinth of tiny streets where abject poverty coexists with vigorous prosperity.

Changing and changeless

The first city here, Indraprashtra, has a semi-mythical status. Some 3000 years old, it is mentioned in the great epic the *Mahabharata*. Archaeologists have identified seven or eight, perhaps even ten, different cities that superseded it, each with a different name. The legacy of this long history is a city dotted with innumerable holy sites, belonging to all the religions, as well as numerous bazaars and a plethora of craft traditions. This ancient dynamism is perhaps also the driving force behind its ceaseless expansion.

Old Delhi has a web of small streets and alleys surrounding the bazaars, and was once girdled by walls pierced with impressive city gates. But it retains a handful of landmarks built on a monumental scale, notably the Red Fort (Lal Qila) and the Jama Masjid, the largest mosque in India. These date from the reign of the Mughal Emperor Shah Jahan, creator of the Taj Mahal, who shifted his capital from Agra to Old Delhi, then called Shahjahanabad. This was the last of the pre-British cities of Delhi.

In 1911 the city was chosen by the British to take over the role of Calcutta as the capital of the

Feeding the capital   *A fruit and vegetable market in Old Delhi.*

colonial empire, and it underwent a renaissance before its inauguration in 1931. Majestic – bombastic even – in its conception, New Delhi was built in a style that drew on Indian, British and classical traditions. The great avenue known as the Rajpath is the ultimate expression of British imperial glory, sweeping majestically from the India Gate (commemorating the 85 000 Indian dead of the First World War), to the Rashtrapati Bhavan (the former residence of the Viceroys, and now the presidential palace).

Ever growing

Delhi became the capital of the world's largest democracy in 1947. The arrival of Sikh and Hindu refugees from the Punjab, which was split in two by Partition, resulted in the creation of the first of a series of new settlements to the south of imperial Delhi, such as Malviya Nagar, Lajpat Nagar, and Rajendra Nagar. To accommodate the growing tide of newcomers (mainly from adjacent states, but also from the rest of India), the city has expanded

Processional way   The India Gate marks the eastern end of the Rajpath.

every year. The government has sought to take drastic measures by demanding the closure of 100 000 polluting factories, but the threatened loss of a million jobs provoked violent protest that brought the city to a standstill for two weeks in December 2000, and forced the government to back down.

Mughal elegance   The Qutb Minar is partly built of red sandstone.

Proclaiming Islam

The Quwwat-ul-Islam Masjid, 10 miles (16 km) south of the centre of New Delhi, was the first major mosque built on Indian soil. It was begun in 1193 by the conqueror Qutb-ud-Din Aybak, who took the name of Sultan of Delhi. As the inscription above its eastern door proclaims, the mosque was built out of material from 27 'idolatrous' Hindu and Jain temples. In so doing, many of the rules of Islam were thrown to the wind: the columns are decorated with figures, including sensuous women. The mosque is dominated by the Qutb Minar, a tower 240 ft (73 m) high; also begun in 1193, it was built to serve as both a minaret and a victory monument.

farther towards the south, gradually absorbing the sites of the ancient capitals. Construction companies built, and continue to build, developments for the wealthy on what was once farmland. Meanwhile, the industrial zones of Noida and Ghaziabad have expanded along the east bank of the River Yamuna.

Some of these new developments are about 12 miles (20 km) from the city centre. Considerable time was needed to cross the intervening distance: the road network has reached saturation point, and the provision of public transport falls way below demand. Meanwhile, the slums, called *jhuggies*, home to the poorest of Delhi's population, have also expanded, and are found in most quarters. To add to Delhi's woes, it is one of the most polluted cities in the world, ranking alongside Mexico City and Peking. Air pollution is believed to be responsible for 10 000 deaths in Delhi

Trendsetter   The tomb of the Mughal Emperor Humayun, built in the middle of the 16th century, served as an inspiration for the architects of the Taj Mahal.

Lahore: vestiges of Mughal splendour

Along with its magnificent architecture, Lahore has preserved its status as the cultural and intellectual capital of Pakistan – despite the turmoil and displacement that followed division of the Punjab in 1947, and the scale of the subsequent influx of rural migrants. With a population of 3 million, it is now Pakistan's second largest city.

Mughal art   Lahore Fort detail

Founded in the 7th century on the River Ravi, Lahore has witnessed the arrival of successive waves of conquerors and kings: Greeks, Afghans, Persians, Turks, Arabs and the British have all left their marks. A jewel in the crown of the Ghaznavids and the Mughals, Lahore ranks among the great cities of Islam. Today, it is a thronging city, with vibrant bazaars, houses decked with ornate balconies, grand mansions and countless mosques, and streets busy with cars, scooters, hand-painted trucks and bullock carts. Its prosperity reflects its status as capital of the Pakistani province of Punjab, the rice and grain basket of the nation. Since independence, it has also developed as an industrial centre, specialising in metalwork, engineering, chemicals, textiles and leatherwork.

of the city, and his wife, Empress Nur Jahan, called it 'another paradise'. Jahangir's son Shah Jahan, creator of the Taj Mahal, was born here. The city was also the capital of the short-lived Sikh kingdom of Ranjit Singh, Maharaja of the Punjab, in the early 19th century, before it fell to the British in 1847. They created tree-lined malls with an imperial flavour, grand buildings in 'Mughal-Gothic' style and a cantonment of comfortable bungalows for their officials. During their era, the city became known as the 'Queen of British India'.

The pearl of the Punjab

Successive rulers have fortified and embellished Lahore and it is one of the greatest centres of Mughal architecture. Akbar the Great made it his capital from 1584 to 1598; he rebuilt the vast Lahore Fort and enclosed the city with a wall. Emperor Jahangir was very fond

Islamic perfection   The Shalimar Gardens

The Shalimar Gardens: tranquil pleasures

The Mughal Emperor Shah Jahan, creator of the Shalimar Gardens, wrote: 'A garden is the purest of human pleasure.' Even though they cover 42 acres (17 ha), they were designed and built in just one year, five months and four days, being completed in 1642. They remain a classic example of Islamic garden design, a combination of water, terraces, pavilions, formal flower beds, fruit trees, lawns and parkland.

To the glory of Islam   The Badshahi Mosque, built by the Mughal Emperor Aurangzeb in 1673, has a vast courtyard, with a capacity for thousands of worshippers.

Karachi: a multifaceted megalopolis

Karachi is Pakistan's largest city and only seaport. Its industrial and financial activities have made it the economic hub, but it also suffers from a lethal crossfire between ethnic, religious, political and criminal rivals.

Cheek by jowl *Multi-storey dwellings with projecting balconies ensure the best use of space in this crowded city.*

In 1800, Karachi was just a small fishing hamlet on the desert coast to the west of the delta of the River Indus. In 1839 the British seized it and the die was cast: they developed it as a port, and later drove railway links up the Indus Valley, creating a conduit for exporting grain and cotton. By the start of the 20th century, Karachi was one of the world's busiest and most modern ports.

Economic giant

At Partition, Karachi was appointed the capital of Pakistan, a status that it kept for 12 years until 1959. It is still the capital of the province of Sindh. Its port activities – also serving landlocked Afghanistan – attracted heavy industries. Producing metals and machinery, textiles and clothing, shoes, petroleum products and chemicals, Karachi now accounts for 60 per cent of the federal government's revenues and 80 per cent of the income of the provincial government, and generates at least 30 per cent of the GNP.

This prosperity has also attracted populations from various parts of the subcontinent. After Partition, *mohajirs* (Indian Muslims) arrived in their millions. They added to a cultural mix consisting of local Sindhis, plus communities from all over Pakistan, as well as Sikhs and Goans, Chinese and Lebanese. After the India-Pakistan War of 1971 and the split with Bangladesh, thousands of Bihari Muslims from Bangladesh arrived, followed ten years later by Afghans escaping the Soviet invasion. Karachi is now the 12th largest city in the world, with a population of 11.8 million.

Buildings do not last much longer than 30 years, with the result that the city is mainly modern and looks like a perpetual building site. Multistorey shopping complexes and new buildings rise from a maze of tiny streets. In the bazaars at street level, dozens of tiny stalls sell thousands of different wares – including locally made carpets and craft goods of beaten copper and brass, lacquered wood and leather.

Visitors to the fishing docks can see the day's catch advertised by the vendors' calls, and watch the huge merchant ships unload their cargoes. This is also the place to buy peculiar fish-based medicines much prized by the *hakims* (local healers).

Cities of Pakistan

[Map showing Afghanistan, Islamabad, Lahore, Pakistan, Indus, New Delhi, Karachi, Arabian Sea, India]

The Karachi mafia: trafficking and violence

Karachi is a liberal city by Islamic standards, but it has an unenviable record for violence and murder. In 1995, 1500 murders were recorded. Inter-ethnic squabbles, petty crime and political assassination take their toll, but the real problem is the ongoing war between gangs controlling the traffic in arms and drugs. The city is a major international hub for narcotics: police estimate that 1.5 million people in Pakistan are addicted to heroin, including 80 000 children.

All hours *A watch shop in Karachi*

Kathmandu: temples at the crossroads

Capital of Nepal since the late 18th century, Kathmandu shares its history with other former capitals lying close by in its valley, Patan and Bhaktapur. All three have ornate Newari architecture and have long served as a meeting point for merchants from Tibet, China and India, and for followers of Hinduism, Buddhism and Islam.

Kathmandu was founded in AD 723, in a valley surrounded by Himalayan peaks, 4300 ft (1310 m) above sea level. The name means 'house of wood', a reference to its oldest temple, Kastamandap, which stands in Durbar Square in the centre of the old city. The temple, made of wood, probably dates back to the 12th century and stands on the site of an earlier structure. In its architecture, as in its daily life, Kathmandu resounds to echoes of the deep past.

Capital of art

The Newars, the original inhabitants of this valley, are famed for their artistic flair. Many of the Newari buildings are made from wood of the sal tree (*Shorea robusta*), and another characteristic material is red brick. Apart from the Kastamandap, Durbar Square contains a number of pagoda-like Hindu temples, with multi-storeyed roofs reminiscent of the mountains.

Close by is the former palace (*durbar*) of the Malla kings, a dynasty that dominated the valley from the 13th to 18th centuries. It is called the Hanuman Dhoka, named after its statue of the Hindu monkey god, which is habitually smeared with red paste and covered with red cloth as an act of courtesy. Narrow alleys lead away from the square, flanked by old buildings of brick and wood with ornately carved balconies and doors and latticework windows. Countless statues delicately sculpted in stone, wall paintings and carved woodwork give the town a distinctive, hand-crafted charm.

Window dressing *Toranas are elaborate pediments found above doors and windows of temples. This example, made of painted wood, adorns the Temple of Ganesha in Durbar Square.*

Crossroads of influences

Nepal is primarily Hindu, and is ruled by the world's only Hindu monarch, who is said to be an incarnation of Vishnu. But many

Woodcarvers' art *The temple of Changu Narayan, or Vishnu, is believed to be the oldest Hindu temple in the Kathmandu Valley, dating back to the 3rd century AD. It is set on a hilltop near Bhaktapur, 8 miles (13 km) east of Kathmandu.*

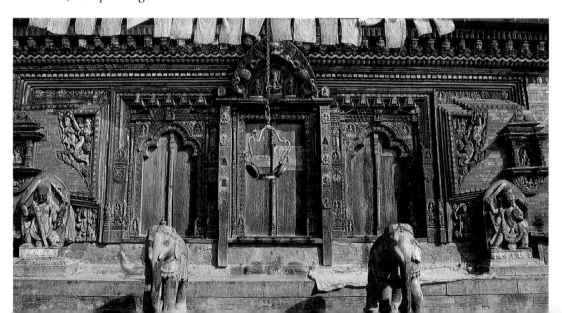

All-seeing, all-knowing *The Stupa of Swayambunath, 2.5 miles (4 km) from the centre of Kathmandu. Above the white dome-like structure, the eyes of Buddha look out to all points of the compass. The current building dates from the 14th century, and is one of many examples in Nepal of the cross-fertilisation of Buddhist and Hindu styles.*

the crown of a hill, is Swayambunath stupa, the oldest Buddhist shrine in the valley, which has a conical tower rising up over a collection of shrines topped by tiered roofs.

Modern times

In 1934 Kathmandu was badly damaged by an earthquake, which claimed more than 4000 lives. Rebuilding provided an opportunity to modernise: new roads have placed Kathmandu, which until recently relied on a network of pathways, at the hub of a national transport system. The airport opened up to international traffic in 1974, and modern suburbs are springing up around the periphery of the city as the population approaches half a million.

Old ways *Tiny shops line the streets of Kathmandu, offering wares ranging from locally made craft goods to imported plastic homewares and cassettes.*

of its ethnic groups are Buddhist. It also has a large number of Tibetan Buddhist refugees, and Muslims. The Kathmandu Valley also has a variety of religions and places of worship.

The most important Hindu shrine in Nepal lies a few miles from Kathmandu, on the banks of the River Bagmati. With its tiered roof covered in gold leaf, the Great Temple of Pashupatinath is dedicated to Pashupati, an incarnation of Shiva unique to Nepal, and its chief deity.

Nearby, the large white dome of the Bodhnath stupa, reached by climbing 600 steps, is the holiest site for the Tibetan Buddhists, who come here during winter pilgrimages. Farther to the west, on

The road to Kathmandu

Beatniks, hippies and junkies have all made their way to Kathmandu. In the late 1960s and early 1970s, amid the gloom cast by the Cold War and the Vietnam War, young Westerners set off by bus and truck along the 'hippie trail' to Southern Asia to seek adventure, enlightenment, or a drug-fuelled paradise. Hanging out on 'Freak Street', they hoped to experience a way of life that better suited their outlook: spiritual, craft-based, in touch with nature, untainted by technology and international commercialism. Turmoil in the Middle East cut off that trail in the early 1980s, and tough new drug laws in Nepal put paid to the easy availability of narcotics. Kathmandu remains a goal for adventurous spirits, but these days the focus is on hill-walking and trekking, and climbing the world's highest peaks. Influenced by exposure to these foreign visitors, the people of Kathmandu have opened their doors to modernisation. Their society has been undergoing rapid change since the 1960s, as they take advantage of the international markets. It is a process of give and take – astutely observed by the British-born Indian writer Pico Iyer in his book *Video Night in Kathmandu* (1988).

Chandigarh: a modern city of a new nation

Built at the start of the post-war era of independence, as the world began to shed its imperial past, Chandigarh was for a long while held to be a vision of Utopia. The new city inspired the dreams of young nations that wanted to shake off the colonial yoke and to begin afresh with a newly forged spirit of modernity.

Desirable residence *Chandigarh is a popular place to live and its people are fiercely proud of their city, which they claim is the cleanest in India.*

The daring initiative that became Chandigarh was launched by the prime minister of India, Jawaharlal Nehru, in 1948. The idea was to create a brand-new city, free of any architectural reference to the past. The result is a city of world renown. It was the last great urban project of the ground-breaking, Swiss-born architect Le Corbusier (1887-1965) and contains the world's largest concentration of his buildings.

Garden of delights *The Nek Chand Rock Garden contains walkways, grottoes and water features, and some 5000 sculptures.*

The chessboard

At Partition, the Punjab was divided between India and Pakistan. Indian Punjab became a state and needed a new capital to serve as the seat of regional administration and to deal with the Sikh and Hindu refugees from Pakistan. A site was chosen on the Punjabi Plain at the base of the Siwalik Hills, between two rivers that had been channelled to feed the artificial Lake Sukhna. A number of international architects were courted for the project, including the American town planner Albert Mayer, who drew up the first sketches, and the Frenchman Auguste Perret. With no preconditions and no jury, the project was open to any sort of architectural fantasy. Finally, in 1951, Le Corbusier accepted the task. Assisted by his cousin Pierre Jeanneret, and by the British partnership of Maxwell Fry and Jane Drew, he laid out a grid pattern, like a chessboard, divided into 46 sectors. In Sector 1 he built the administrative quarter; in 10 the museums; in 14 the university; in 16 the Rose Garden; in 17 the city centre, with a large commercial complex. The other sectors contain identically-styled blocks of flats, two or three storeys high, and generous amounts of green space and lakes. Broad, cross-town boulevards distribute the road traffic. Many of the building are raised on pilotis, the reinforced concrete columns that were Le Corbusier's trademark. He also designed most of the public buildings, notably the Legislative Assembly and the High Court.

Wear and tear

As industry is prohibited, the city suffers little pollution, but its concrete has discoloured badly with age. Moreover, although the city was originally designed for 500 000 people, it now contains nearly a million, and many areas of unused land have been claimed by squatters from the countryside. Such factors have undermined the tidy, Utopian effect of the original vision. Nonetheless, Chandigarh, now joint capital of Punjab and Haryana, is popularly considered a great success.

20th-century classic *The Legislative Assembly (or Vidhan Sabha) was designed by Le Corbusier, whose work after the Second World War became increasingly sculptural.*

Madras: easy-going affluence

With about 6 million inhabitants, the city of Madras – or Chennai, as it now prefers to be called – is the fourth largest city in India and the capital of Tamil Nadu. Its historical importance and economic self-sufficiency have imbued it with a strong sense of identity, reinforced by its language, Tamil, and its Dravidian culture.

Days off *On public holidays, thousands head for the city's beaches.*

Madras began as a collection of villages set around the little fishing port of Madraspatnam. In 1639 the East India Company set up a trading post here, and in 1653 built Fort St George. The town, known by the shortened name of Madras, developed in competition with the French port of Pondicherry, and its position was enhanced by the military campaigns of Robert Clive in the mid-18th century. It then became an important centre of imperial administration and built a powerful economic base founded on cotton and textiles.

The art of living in an industrial centre

Madras has undergone massive growth since independence, but it has been spared many of the problems of rapid urban development and the scourge of endemic poverty. Its calm, almost languid atmosphere is credited to its position on the Coromandel Coast, freshened by the sea breezes, albeit these days tainted with pollution.

The sea also accounts for much of its economic success. Madras is not only a major port, with its large artificial harbour, but also an industrial centre, producing petrochemicals, cars, electronic equipment, railway equipment, and much more.

Advertising billboards encourage consumer spending. Many of the posters draw attention to another of Madras's claims to fame as the country's second most active producer of films, after Mumbai. But in Madras, the films are in Tamil; in Mumbai they are in Hindi. Film stars play a major role in public life in Madras.

The screen idol M.G. Ramachandran (fondly known as MGR) was active in politics for 25 years before his own party, the AIADMK, was elected to power in 1977 and he became Chief Minister of Tamil Nadu. A populist also known for his hardline attitude to dissent, he was re-elected for three consecutive terms and remained in power for 11 years. When he died in 1987, 2 million people attended his funeral procession. Other popular actors have followed his example.

Madras prides itself on its intellectual and cultural prestige: its universities have a high reputation across India, while its Festival of Carnatic (South Indian) Music and Dance, held between mid-December and mid-January, is one of the largest of its kind in the world.

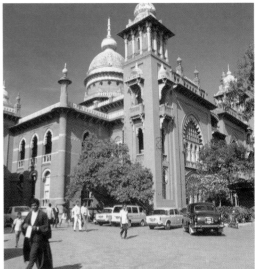

The full weight of the law *The High Court, built in Mughal style in 1892, is one of the world's largest palaces of justice.*

Early Christian remains *The Catholic cathedral of San Thome, rebuilt at the end of the 19th century, claims to house the relics of Saint Thomas the Apostle.*

111

Calcutta: capital of culture

With some 13 million inhabitants, the capital of West Bengal, situated on a branch of the Ganges Delta, serves as a gateway to the most heavily populated region of the Indian world. Despite its superb monuments, which bear witness to a prestigious colonial past, Calcutta is more usually associated with the rash of vast slum areas in which one-third of the city's population lives.

Since August 24, 1999, Calcutta has been officially known as Kolkata: the Indian government hopes thereby to underline the 'Indianisation' of this former capital of British India. Its centre remains nonetheless very English: the Victoria Memorial, a supreme example of colonial architecture, the huge Fort William, and the National Library (the largest in India) recall the epoch when Calcutta was at the heart of the colonial empire.

A British trading station

Calcutta was founded by the British three centuries ago. In 1686 an English merchant called Job Charnock persuaded his colleagues to set up a trading port on this site. The early decades were blighted by raids; in one raid, in 1756, the town was captured by the Nawab of Bengal and 123 British captives suffocated in a tiny guardroom, the infamous 'Black Hole of Calcutta'. Robert Clive retook the town the following year and won the decisive Battle of Plassey, which firmly established the British hold over India. Calcutta became the capital of British India, and grew on an imperial scale, with administrative buildings, educational institutes, churches, private palaces, museums and botanical gardens. By 1911, when Delhi became the new imperial capital, Calcutta was handling 60 per cent of British business in India. Jute manufactured in the surrounding region, coal, tea from Assam, any goods produced in significant quantity, were brought to the port that stretched along the course of the River Hugli (or Hooghly).

Intellectual crucible

Besides this commercial wealth, Calcutta also developed an intellectual tradition. Its universities provide a large proportion of the nation's elite, and are known for their political engagement. This being a Marxist-dominated corner of India, they are still plastered with portraits of Marx, Engels and Lenin. Calcutta's distinctly Bengali culture has also fostered numerous artists, musicians and writers, including the poet Rabindranath Tagore, and the film director Satyajit Ray. Local cinema production is markedly different from that of Mumbai (Bombay): Calcutta is the capital of India's art-house movies.

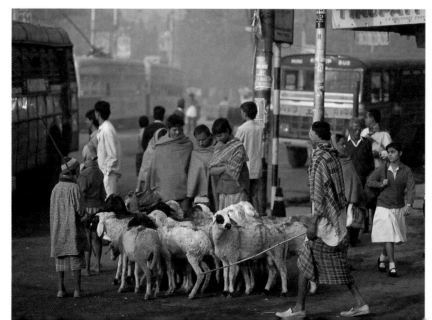

Harsh realities
Thousands of people from rural areas come to Calcutta in the hope of finding work and end up living in wretched conditions. A poster in a slum underlines the gap between image and reality.

Commuting *Goats travel by bus to the outskirts of the city to graze.*

The poverty of the slums

Calcutta suffers acute urban deprivation. Massive overcrowding has been exacerbated by deficient infrastructure: the provision of water and electricity is patchy, and road transport is chaotic. But such conditions are Calcutta's historic legacy. Rudyard Kipling found conditions so shocking in the colonial heyday that he wrote *The City of Dreadful Night* (1890). The situation worsened with the collapse of the jute industry, the

Images of the gods   Kumartuli is the sculptors' quarter.

decline of the port and a runaway increase in population, swelled by the arrival of huge numbers of refugees at Partition in 1947, and then during the creation of Bangladesh in 1971.

Mother Teresa

It was her first-hand experience of these frightful living conditions, and the sight of so many poor dying on the streets, that persuaded the Albanian nun Agnes Gonxha Bojaxhiu, better known as Mother Teresa, to found her Order of Missionaries of Charity in 1948. In addition to the Hospital for the Dying Destitute, a leprosy clinic and an orphanage, the missionaries have opened refuges for the down-and-out. The work of Mother Teresa took on an international dimension when, denouncing the slums that have grown up in all the big cities of the developing world, she presided over the inauguration of similar refuges around the globe. She received the Nobel peace prize in 1979, and died in 1997 aged 87.

There is still plenty of work for the Missionaries of Charity and other organisations to do, but in truth, conditions in modern Calcutta are not much worse than in many other Indian cities. The city's achievements, such as its efficient underground railway system (the first in India), tend to be eclipsed by its old reputation as a site of human degradation.

The delights of Darjeeling

A splendid summer station, offering an escape from the heat and humidity of the Indian plains, Darjeeling is perched on a mountain ridge at 7050 ft (2150 m) above sea level in the far north of West Bengal. It was originally a Buddhist settlement called Dorje Ling, 'Place of the Thunderbolt', but the modern town was founded by the British in the middle of the 19th century as a summer retreat for troops and the government of Bengal. It has now become a holiday resort boasting some 200 hotels, catering for both Indians and foreigners. Darjeeling is also the gateway to neighbouring Sikkim, and the starting point for treks and assaults on Kangchenjunga (28 165 ft/8585 m), the world's third highest summit, which lies in view of the town. Darjeeling tea, rated as among the best in the world, is grown on 80 estates or 'gardens'. Most of the 40 000 tea workers are Nepali-speaking, descended from the Gurkha immigrants; discrimination by government has goaded them into sometimes violent rebellion in recent years. But Darjeeling is also a place of contemplation, as evidenced by the saffron robes of Buddhists attending the handful of monasteries, or *gompas*, and strolling around the town.

Going with the flow   The Howrah Bridge across the River Hugli.

113

CHAPTER 5

CULTURE AND TRADITIONS

For more than 3500 years, Indian culture has been continuously influenced by foreign occupation, and refined by a process of selection and assimilation. Indian sculpture, for example, went through a radical transformation when Buddhist monks adopted the more realistic, three-dimensional style of the Greeks, which had spread to adjacent empires after the conquests of Alexander the Great. The Muslims were responsible for widespread destruction of ancient Hindu and Buddhist monuments, but they brought their own stylistic panache to their mosques, fortresses and palaces. Through synthesis with Persian, Arab and Indian styles, this came into full flourish under the Mughal emperors. Under the British, the subcontinent was exposed to the European approach to art, literature and theatre, and nowhere is this more apparent today than in the world of Indian cinema.

Art is closely linked to religion, as seen here at the Swaminarayan Temple at Bhuj in Gujarat.

Indian festivals: the gods enjoy them, too

Just about every day of the year there is a festival of some kind in Southern Asia, held in honour of one of the numerous deities, saints and prophets. Many of these events are small, village affairs, but some are on a grand scale. All demonstrate the vitality of religious devotion across the subcontinent, and the way in which the sacred permeates all aspects of everyday life.

Demon dancer   *Crowds are entertained by a costumed dancer, impersonating a god, at Lamayuru, an ancient Buddhist monastery in Ladakh, in the Himalayas of India.*

The majority of Hindu festivals take place during the summer monsoon season, between June/July and October/November, for at this time the gods are said to be resting: Vishnu has retired to his subterranean realm accompanied by a retinue of other gods, leaving the world vulnerable to danger, which needs to be averted by festivities. As Vishnu is also the protector of newly-weds, marriages tend not to take place at this time, but during the cooler months between November and March.

The four great Hindu festivals

During the monsoon months, four major festivals take place, each originally associated with specific castes, but now celebrated more widely. Shravan Purnima was a Brahman festival; Dussehra was associated with the Durga-worhip of the Kshatriyas; Divali was celebrated particularly by the Vaisyas. Holi, the main Sudra festival, takes place in February/March and marks the return of spring.

Shravan Purnima is held at the full moon (*purnima*) at the end of the month of Sravana (July/August). On this day, after performing purifying ablutions and rituals in the waters of a holy river, high-caste men

change the sacred threads they wear from their left shoulder. These rituals also coincide with Raksha Bandhan, the festival of brothers and sisters: sisters tie an amulet (*raksha*), such as a cotton bracelet dipped in turmeric, around the wrist of their brothers, to protect them from witchcraft and the Evil Eye; in return, the brothers present their sisters with gifts and vow to protect them during the coming year.

Festival of the warrior caste

Dussehra is also known as the 'victory of the tenth day'. It commemorates the victory of Rama, hero of the *Ramayana*, over the demon Ravana,

Monsoon joy

The arrival of the monsoon rains is greeted with celebration in India. As the winds change direction, they bring moisture-laden air from the ocean, putting an end to the oppressive heat of summer. But the celebrations are not simply about physical comfort, for the monsoon also marks the beginning of the agricultural year. The survival of most of the people on the subcontinent depends on the rains, and they do not forget this in their prayers.

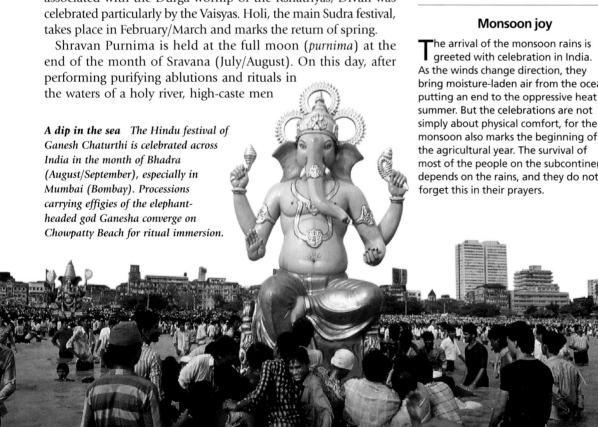

A dip in the sea   *The Hindu festival of Ganesh Chaturthi is celebrated across India in the month of Bhadra (August/September), especially in Mumbai (Bombay). Processions carrying effigies of the elephant-headed god Ganesha converge on Chowpatty Beach for ritual immersion.*

Candle power *During Divali, the 'Festival of Lights', candles are placed on miniature rafts and floated onto water. The lights of Divali are said to light the path for Lakshmi, goddess of wealth.*

and takes place in the month of Asvina (September/October). The festival reaches its crescendo when giant effigies of Ravana, made of wood and paper, are burnt on pyres.

Dussehra follows Navratri, the 'Festival of Nine Nights' dedicated to the goddess Durga. In some regions, women observe a daytime fast for the duration. In West Bengal, this is the time of Durga Puja, when homage is paid to the goddess Durga, killer of demons. All over Calcutta temporary shrines are erected, made of bamboo draped with white cloth, to house large effigies of Durga. On the fourth day the idols are immersed in the sacred water of the River Hugli, a branch of the Ganges.

The festival of the merchants

Divali, or Deepavali, takes place over several days in the month of Kartika (October/November). This coincides with the last days of the traditional financial year, as celebrated by the Vaisya merchant caste. Shops are cleaned and redecorated, inventories are taken, and devotions are paid to Lakshmi, goddess of wealth, good fortune and beauty. In this spirit of renewal, a family will also whitewash the house, repaint the front door, springclean the interior, and pay off debts. They put on new clothes, and in the evening light oil lamps and candles. Throughout the festival, children let off fireworks, and the nights are filled with music, shows, processions and parties. This is also a festival of sweets, which are exchanged as gifts.

Holi is a festival of exuberant, almost anarchic fun. In a carnival atmosphere, people wander the street throwing coloured powder at each other, or squirting one another with syringes filled with coloured liquid. Brahman priests dowse the crowds around the temples dedicated to Krishna, the much loved god who, it is said, enjoyed playing this paint-splashing game with the *gopis* (herdswomen or milkmaids). The festival is associated with the divine lover Krishna, and the god of love, Kama.

Primary colour *The dominant colour in the dye-throwing festival of Holi is red. This is said to symbolise new blood and the regeneration that occurs in spring. It is not the time to wear one's best clothes.*

Dance: a sacred art

Of the seven countries of the subcontinent, India is unquestionably the most richly endowed with traditions of dance. While popular folk dancing expresses a natural joy in movement, temple dancing is a highly refined art form, with profound sacred significance.

In character *A Kathakali dancer applies his make-up. This form of dance-theatre from Kerala re-enacts scenes from the great Hindu epics.*

According to Hindu myth, dance was at the very origin of the Universe, performed by Shiva Nataraja, the Cosmic Dancer. This art, which has its roots in ancient cultural tradition, is a central feature of many festivals and ceremonies, and even today is surrounded by an aura of sanctity.

Techniques created by the gods

A common thread of spirituality links all forms of Hindu dancing. It is said Brahma himself composed the *Natya Veda* ('knowledge of dancing'), which he revealed to the sage Bharatamuni in about 200 BC so that he could teach a style of dancing that would please and entertain the gods. Shiva was so pleased with the results that he commanded his attendant, the musician Tandu, to initiate the sage in the technique of the *tandava*, the cosmic dance of creation and destruction, which is associated also with fertility and masculinity, while his wife Parvati taught him the gentler *lasya*. Bharatamuni, inspired by his divine teachers, was able to compose his celebrated treatise on dance and music called *Natya-Shastra*, the foundation stone upon which the art and technique of classical Hindu dancing rests.

This tradition has been passed down for more than 2000 years. From a tender age, novice dancers learn how to exploit the potential for movement of all parts of their body, a process that requires dedicated practice over many years. Following strictly defined movements, they use their bodies, in particular their eyes and hands, to portray a variety of sacred symbols. *Mudras*, sacred signs made by gestures of the hands, fingers and arms, are particularly significant. All movement has to be perfectly coordinated with the music, creating a seamless harmony.

Dancing for the gods In the past, female dancers belonged to the temples and were called deva-dasi, 'servants of the gods'. Educated within the temple from a young age, they formed their own caste and were governed by strict rules.

Fingers and toes *Examples of* Barata-Natyam *gestures, as taught by the Madras school of dance.*

Classical dance

The main styles of classical dancing are all concerned with presenting stories about the gods, often tales from the great epics, the *Ramayana* and *Mahabharata*, as well as love stories, such as that of Krishna and Radha, as told in the *Gitagovinda* ('Song of the Cowherd'). While the techniques were all originally inspired by the words of Bharatamuni, there are significant regional differences in performance, seen in the style of dancing and the main themes presented, as well as in the costumes and make-up.

The most famous form of classical Indian dance is undoubtedly the *Bharata-Natyam*, which originated in southern India; Tanjore (Tanjavur) and Madras (Chennai) remain prestigious centres of excellence. A dancer, usually female and dancing alone on stage, plays the part of dozens of characters in a single performance, combining three choreographic elements: pure dance or *nritta*, based on the rhythm and geometry of her movements in space; *nritya*, which combines emotional expression with symbolic gesture; and *natya*, the danced drama.

Kathakali (literally, 'story play') is a kind of stylised theatrical performance from the south-western coast of India, notably Kerala. The performers – traditionally male, wearing wide skirts and huge headdresses, their faces plastered with make-up – act out stories in dance-like mime, to the accompaniment of singing and music. Performances sometimes last the entire night, lit dramatically by large oil lamps.

Kathak, a style of dance from northern India, reflects Persian and Islamic influences. It was popular at the Mughal court, and costumes still echo 17th-century styles. It is best known for the drumbeat sound produced by the footwork, and the highly controlled ringing of anklet bells. *Manipuri* is a delicate, flowing style of classical dance practised in the north-east. *Kuchipudi*, from Andhra Pradesh, dates from the 17th century, while *Odissi* is thought to be the oldest of all the classical dance forms.

Sound and movement *The Hindu festival of Dussehra is the occasion for this exuberant dance, performed to the beat of percussion music.*

Masters of disguise *The theyyams of northern Kerala are one of the most spectacular manifestations of folk art in India. There are more than 370 different* theyyam *dances, each representing a god or a hero, and each with a very elaborate costume. The performers are male and conduct their trance-like feats of movement and endurance to the sound of drums and horns.*

Music from the heavens

Like dance, music has religious significance. According to Indian tradition, it comes from the heavens, and has the power to exorcise malevolent forces. But it also expresses the rhythms and colours of the subcontinent.

In Hindu legend, the gods were churning the thousands of stars in order to find the nectar of immortality when a foul venom spurted from the mouth of the cosmic serpent, which they were using as a rope, and nearly destroyed the whole of Creation. Shiva swallowed the poison and the orchestra of the gods – consisting of the flute, the lute and percussion – struck up in order to annihilate its evil powers. In both India and Sri Lanka, music and dance are thought capable of invoking the power and blessings of the gods, as well as conjuring up demons.

Melody and rhythm

Two styles dominate traditional music. The Hindustani music of the north has much in common with the classical music of Pakistan and shows many signs of Persian influence. In the south, Carnatic music (meaning 'from southern India') bears fewer marks of outside influence and observes stricter rules. Both are played by small groups of around six musicians and use similar – but different – instruments, mixing a variety of strings with flute, tabla and other expressive drums, and sometimes voice. The sitar, with its 100 strings, for instance, is essentially a Hindustani instrument, whereas the seven-stringed vina is associated with Carnatic music. In both styles, a constant background drone sound is provided by the stringed instrument called a tambura. And both forms are characterised in large measure by the subtle impact of the *raga* (the theoretical melodic shape) and the *tala* (rhythmic metre), which create the overlapping repetition that makes Indian music so distinctive.

Singing for his supper   A baul is an itinerant bard who travels around Bengal performing poems to the accompaniment of an ektar, a one-stringed violin.

Through its microtonal fluctuations, the *raga* casts the mood and expresses the nine fundamental emotions prescribed by Sanskrit poetry. Five to seven notes (from the 12-note octave scale) determine the character of the melody. Each *raga* has a particular tonality associated with an hour of the day or night. The idea of performing a morning *raga* at 10 o'clock at night seems absurd to an Indian musician, which makes the rigid scheduling of Western concerts hard to accommodate. *Ragas* may also correspond to a god, a colour, or to a particular season or planetary alignment. With virtually no musical notations, they are passed down orally from master to pupil, who both jealously guard their particular

How the sage Narada learnt true music

The great sage Narada claimed to be the greatest of all musicians and boasted about it to the gods. Shiva and Vishnu were not impressed and decided to teach him a lesson. They led him to a huge building filled with crying men and women. They were *ragas* and *raginis* (the feminine equivalent of *ragas*), whose arms and legs had been broken by Narada's playing and singing, and they had been condemned to remain in this state of wounded anguish until they were correctly sung. This the goddess Saraswati duly did, and she restored the captives to health. Narada acknowledged his inadequacies and his arrogance, and implored the gods to teach him to play better. He later became priest to the musicians of the gods.

Food of love   In a 19th-century painting, Krishna is shown playing a flute to charm the shepherdesses.

outlines for the *ragas* in their repertoire; these give them the framework upon which to improvise.

The *tala*, the rhythmic metre, provides another key element; it remains unchanged for the duration of the *raga*. The rhythm of Hindu music is derived from the metres found in Sanskrit poetry and is beaten out in a succession of long and short syllables. *Tala* means 'palm of the hand', and this is what traditionally marked the rhythm, although these days drums are more prominent.

The sound of India *Ravi Shankar and his daughter Anoushka play the sitar at a music festival in Mumbai (Bombay). Ravi Shankar brought the subtlety of Indian music to world attention during the 1960s and 1970s.*

Drum roll *Women beat out the rhythm at the Esala Perahera, the great 10-day festival of Kandy, Sri Lanka, held in honour of the precious relic of the Buddha, the Sacred Tooth.*

Nusrat Fateh Ali Khan, 'The Brightest Star' of Sufi music

The great Pakistani singer Nusrat Fateh Ali Khan died in London on August 16, 1997, at the age of 49. Also a composer and teacher, he was one of the most famous of all singers of Sufi devotional music (*qawwals*). A versatile musician, he had a gift for mixing jazz and techno with the *qawwal* tradition, producing hypnotic rhythms with profoundly spiritual overtones. Nusrat also wrote music for Indian cinema and for international movies, including Martin Scorsese's *Last Temptation of Christ*, and Tim Robbins' *Dead Man Walking*.

Sufi music is played by groups of three to 13 male musicians, and it is characterised by the use of strong voices, solo or in unison, and repetition and improvisation. Drumming and hand-clapping also play a prominent role. A piece begins with an instrumental prelude played on a harmonium, followed by a poem (the *ruba'i*), performed as a recitative by the soloist without percussion accompaniment; then the singing begins. Orthodox Islam does not countenance any form of sacred music, but Sufis preserve their tradition of worship through music. By listening to this music, the devotee can reaffirm bonds with his spiritual mentor, with the saints, and ultimately with God.

Theatre: ancient and modern

The theatre is a lively art form in both India and Pakistan. Contemporary producers stick close to the traditions of popular theatre and often combine music, dance and mime with the spoken word. The performers have an intimate rapport with their audiences and captivate them with a startling range of work, from quick-silver political satire to masked dramas of mesmeric beauty.

Dramatic impact Theyyam, *the ritualistic folk theatre of northern Kerala, demonstrates vividly the Indian instincts for theatrical effect and sumptuous spectacle.*

No holds are barred in Indian theatre. Traditional plays – usually based on tales from the great epics, the *Mahabharata* and the *Ramayana*, or historical legends – may contain music, dance, acrobatics, stilt-walking and wildly imaginative costume.

Codification and self-expression

Most of the theatrical arts have their roots in the same authority upon which traditional dance is based: the *Natya-Shastra*. This Sanskrit text, dating from about 200 BC, lays down rules governing the costumes, masks, bodily gestures, facial expressions and movement around the stage. It states that, in a single performance, the audience should be made to feel all nine of the following emotions (the *nava rasas*): serenity, valour, anger, laughter, sympathy, disgust, awe, fear and love. The golden age of classical Sanskrit theatre lasted until about 1000 years ago. It had two aims: to entertain and educate the audience, and to please the gods. To this end, performances were always introduced with a prayer. Since then, theatre has drifted more towards popular entertainment, but Sanskrit *kudiyattam* theatre from Kerala has maintained its religious function. It includes one of the key characters in Indian traditional culture – *vidushaka*, who plays a clown-like attendant to the heroes, and comments on the action to the audience.

Puppet parts *This Delhi family have made puppet heads their speciality.*

Ganesha and friends *String puppets made in the Kathmandu Valley perpetuate the close bonds between theatre and religion.*

As with dance and music, Indian theatre is said to have been originated by the gods. According to legend, the god Indra led a group of other gods to plead with Brahma, Creator of the Universe, to provide some kind of creative distraction to save the human race from descent into slovenly ways. Brahma came up with a combination of four elements: speech, song, mime and sentiment. Early Indian theatre was inextricably linked with dancing; indeed, the term *natya* is variously translated as 'dancing' and 'drama'.

Street theatre *A marionette show on the streets of Delhi, accompanied by a harmonium and drums, will always draw a large crowd, and particularly children. The Hindu epics usually provide the storyline.*

Theatre in the struggle for independence

So-called 'modern' theatre arrived in Bengal in the 18th century. British colonialism and world trade provided new sources of inspiration to Bengali writers and performers, notably in Calcutta. These artists created a synthesis between Western traditions and their own theatrical heritage. Many abandoned religious and folkloric subject matter in favour of political works commenting on the British occupation of their land. During the 19th century a similar development took place in Mumbai: there, the Parsees established a modern tradition of theatre, written in Gujarati, Hindi or Urdu, which, by touring widely, sent ripples right across the north and west of the country. Bengali and Parsee drama breathed new life into Indian theatre and is still appreciated, both in India and abroad.

Puppets and the strings of destiny

In the subcontinent, puppets can achieve extraordinary feats and are quite capable of recounting entire epics on a mammoth scale and staging apocalyptic battles. Rajasthan could claim to have the most famous and respected heritage in marionettes (string puppets). Called *kathputhilis*, they are made of wood and gloriously clothed. The puppeteers are all men: women are excluded from the profession. The equally famous leather cut-out puppets of Andhra Pradesh, by contrast, are manipulated not by strings but sticks. Kerala has a tradition of glove puppets.

Actors: a caste of nomads

Traditional theatre is a male preserve in India. Skills are passed from father to son and remain within specific castes that permit public performance. Performances can be extremely long (often lasting more than six hours), perhaps spread over several nights, and take place in the open air. Troupes of actors tour the country for months at a time, leading a nomadic existence and sharing the road with other itinerant performers, such as jugglers, acrobats, stilt walkers and mime artists. Topical contemporary plays are popular and will include wry or hilarious comment on events in the news, such as the marriage problems of the British royal family.

123

A long literary tradition

India has one of the world's oldest traditions of literature. Essentially religious in origin, it is remarkable both for its epic scale and the profundity of its philosophy. Latterly, a large number of modern Indian authors have also earned worldwide respect for their work in English.

The history of Indian literature begins with the *Vedas*. Sacred texts composed by the ancient Brahmans between 2000 and 1000 BC, these are books of knowledge, containing hymns to the gods, sacred formulae, liturgical music, myths and legends. From the outset, Indian literature presented a heady mix that exploited to the full the power of human wisdom and imagination.

The oldest philosophical tracts in India are the *Upanishads*, composed between the 8th and 4th centuries BC, and considered as epilogues to the *Vedas*. Exploring the way in which the soul of the individual (*atman*) is identified with the universal soul (*brahman*), they provide the foundation for much of Hindu philosophy. The two great epics of Hindu literature, the *Mahabharata* and the *Ramayana*, date from the 2nd to 1st century BC. Sparkling with genius, these colossal poems also serve as manuals of Hindu social traditions and ethics. They were composed first in Sanskrit, but over the centuries were translated into most Indian languages.

New directions

Hindu literature remained closely bound to religion until the 4th century AD, when the great dramatist and lyric poet Kalidasa developed lighter and more popular forms. This permitted the evolution of drama, comedy, social satire, erotic texts (including the *Kama-Sutra*, the classic Hindu book on love-making and social behaviour, written in the 4th century), folktales and fables (such as the *Pancatantra* collection) in which animals take the lead roles. The Mughal emperors, who were great patrons of the arts, fostered court literature. Writers of the Delhi School, notably Khwaja Mir Daud, Mirza Sauda and Mir Taqi Mir, wrote classical couplet poetry called *ghazals* of great accomplishment and range, including biting satire, and thus helped to sharpen the Indian art of verbal dexterity.

After British colonisation, Indian culture came into contact with modern Western literature. The major Indian languages have their own literary traditions reaching back 500 years or more, and these continue to thrive today. But English has also spread across the country as the language of the educated classes.

Nobel laureate Rabindranath Tagore *wrote in Bengali, but translated his work into English himself.*

The world's longest poem

The *Mahabharata*, 'Tale of the Great Bharatas', is an epic, comparable in both its scope and poetry to Homer's *Iliad* and *Odyssey*. It tells the tale of two sets of warring brothers from related princely families, the Kauravas and the Pandavas. There are countless subplots, myths and legends, swelling the total to 110000 couplets, which makes the *Mahabharata* the world's longest poem. It also contains the famous philosophical work the *Bhagavad Gita*, delivered as a pre-battle dialogue between the god Krishna and Arjuna, one of the Pandava brothers. Created in the 1st millennium BC, it was orally transmitted for more than 2000 years, and was not printed until the 19th century.

भीम   नकुळा   सहदेव   અર્જુન   युधिष्ठिर

Heroic figures The Pandava brothers of the Mahabharata *appear in all art forms.*

Epic clash An 18th-century Indian miniature, depicting a scene from the Ramayana, *shows the ten-headed, 20-armed demon Ravana in combat with the vulture king Jatayu.*

Voice of the diaspora Vidiadhar Surajprasad Naipaul came to international notice with The Mystic Masseur *(1957), set in the Indian community of Trinidad.*

Writing in English

The first major Indian works of fiction and poetry written in the English language appeared under the banner of Anglo-Indian romanticism. They came from writers such as Toru Dutt, Sri Aurobindo and – most celebrated of all – Rabindranath Tagore, who won the Nobel prize for literature in 1913. Mulk Raj Anand, born in 1905, made a deep impression in the first half of the 20th century with his novels about the caste system, such as *Coolie* and *Untouchable*. In the 1940s the struggle for independence was accompanied by a flourish of social and political writings, by such figures as Kasturi Ranga Iyengar and, of course, Gandhi and Nehru. They were followed in the mid-20th century by a number of authors and poets of international reputation, such as Dom Moraes, Nissim Ezekiel and Kamala Das.

A number of Indian authors – or authors of Indian origin – writing in English have served to place Indian literature at the forefront of modern literature and have engendered a greater awareness of their land and culture. They include Nirad Chaudhuri, R.K. Narayan, V.S. Naipaul, Salman Rushdie, Anita Desai, Vikram Seth, Rohinton Mistry and Arundhati Roy, to name but a few.

Ecological activist Booker Prize winner in 1997, Arundhati Roy has since devoted her energies to fighting the construction of the Narmada Dam.

Pile them high A stand at the 13th New Delhi World Book Fair, the biggest in Asia, shows the public thirst for literature in the subcontinent.

The lure and power of Indian cinema

Since the first Indian feature film, Raja Harishchandra, *came out in 1913, India has produced more than 30 000 movies, and now produces more films a year than any other country in the world, including the USA.*

Hollywood produces about 570 movies a year; India produces about 850. As a result, India's leading centre of film production, Mumbai (Bombay), has been given the jokey nickname 'Bollywood'. Its productivity was, if anything, even greater in the past: during the 1980s, it was producing almost twice as many films each year as Hollywood. Bollywood today is the epicentre of Hindi film-making, but the Tamil-language films of Madras and the Telugu-language films of Hyderabad have begun to chip away at Bollywood's dominant role.

Pulling power Huge and vivid film posters are an essential feature of the urban landscape of India. They vie for their share of the 10 million cinema tickets sold daily.

Film spice

Bollywood films are called *masala*, 'mixed spice'. They aim to deliver a powerful mixture of sensations, including slushy love stories, car chases, gun battles, bare-fist fights, rape, kidnap – all carefully choreographed to music. And often the goodies and the baddies will suddenly abandon their hot pursuits in favour of a grand-scale dance sequence, performed to Indian-style pop music. They are not openly spicy in the sensual sense, because Indian censorship holds the film industry on a close rein. Nonetheless, love is a key theme, and eroticism, albeit fully clothed, permeates many Bollywood movies, especially in the dance sequences.

But what really brings spice to popular Indian movies is the audience. The huge queues outside cinemas are an indication of the enthusiasm of the

ticket-holders inside. The action on screen is greeted with a barrage of comments, heckling, laughter and joshing between rival supporters, very much in the tradition of popular theatre. Indeed, the banter from the audience is frequently more entertaining than the filmscript. As for the stars, they are treated as demi-gods, and are richly rewarded. Amitabh Bachchan, recently dubbed 'superstar of the millennium', can earn 30 million rupees (about $620 000) for a single movie.

Dodgy money

Actors' pay can consume one-third of the budget for a film, but commercial success is by no means guaranteed. Indeed, only 20 per cent of *masala* films make any profit at all. But Indian films are not constrained by economic reality; their finances are something of a mystery. For over a decade, the police have accused Bollywood of being a centre for money laundering, while the producers complain

Art cinema and the cost of courage

Not all Indian films appeal to popular taste: movies of profound and delicate observation are also produced. The leading figure in this arena was Satyajit Ray, who received an Oscar in 1992, shortly before his death, for his Lifetime Achievement. Such movies are low budget compared to mainstream films, and they deal with uncomfortable issues, such as social deprivation and political corruption. Mira Nair won the Palme d'Or at Cannes in 1989 for her film about street children *Salaam Bombay!*; eight years later she did battle with the censors over her *Kama-Sutra: A Tale of Love*. In 2000 Deepa Mehta had to abandon shooting *Water*, a film about the plight of Hindu widows, after violent Hindu protests in Varanasi.

Leading light Satyajit Ray directs the action on the set of his 1989 film **Ganashatru** *(Enemy of the People).*

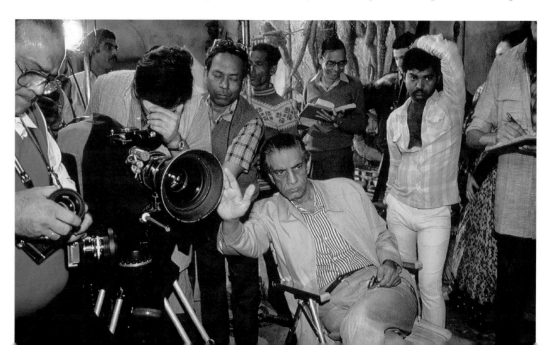

On film Photo-shoot at the Evernew film studios in Lahore, Pakistan.

they are victims of racketeering. Police statistics would suggest that both are the case: they claim that 10 per cent of film production in Mumbai is funded by money-laundering, and 40 per cent of turn-over is used to pay off the mafia.

As if to confirm this murky picture, five producers were assassinated between 1995 and 2000, making the reality of film production in Mumbai seem almost as wild and dangerous as the fiction on screen. Reality also eclipsed fiction in 2000 when Rajkumar, a leading idol of southern Indian cinema and star of over 200 films, was kidnapped by India's most-wanted bandit and held for three months before being released.

Film as cultural bonding

Through its immense mass appeal, cinema has been able to reinforce a sense of unity and solidarity within the Indian nation. The film stars seem to appeal to a broad range of fans. In addition to this, film has given the international community a window on Indian culture: Bollywood films, with increasingly sophisticated production values, have extended their global reach and are exported widely, especially to Britain and Europe, and also to Russia and the rest of Asia. Indian soldiers serving for the UN in Cambodia in 1992 were surprised at their warm reception until they discovered that it was in large part due to the popularity of Indian films there. The Indian military responded by mounting daily *masala* film shows, free of charge and open to all – thus using film not only as a means of bridging cultural gaps, but also as an instrument of peace.

Heart-throb Workers in Calcutta install a vast hoarding to announce the release, in September 2000, of Fiza, featuring Hrithik Roshan, one of the hottest of the new generation of film idols.

Worth the wait Fans wait patiently in a long queue to see an 'all India premiere' of Mani Ratnam's Bombay (1995). Indian cinemas, containing 700-800 seats, are regularly filled to capacity.

Masterpieces of Indian art

Since antiquity, the subcontinent has produced a succession of outstanding works of art in a huge variety of forms and styles. Most of them, however, convey both a deep devotion to the gods and a powerful sensuality. As in all the arts, religion was the inspiration, and artists for the most part remained anonymous.

Gentle pursuits *A miniature of the Pahari school, dating from about 1800, depicts leisure time.*

The tumultuous history of India, a country repeatedly invaded by foreign armies bringing fresh cultural influences, goes a long way towards explaining the diversity of Indian art – and also why comparatively few works have survived. Thus the heyday of the Mughal era (1526-1707), while celebrated for the treasures it created, such as the Taj Mahal, was also responsible for the destruction of countless Hindu, Jain and Buddhist temples. Monuments spared from this desecration, such as the temples of Khajuraho and the caves of Ellora and Ajanta, give us some idea of the marvels that were found across India prior to Muslim times.

Sculpture to the fore

As with many ancient civilisations, sculpture dominates the early history of Indian art, largely because of the durability of stone. Only traces

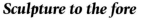

Flower power *A 5th- or 6th-century mural from Ajanta illustrates the bodhisattva Padmapani ('lotus holder').*

remain of other more perishable art forms that may be equally old, but have disappeared through deterioration or deliberate destruction. The legacy of stone sculpture on the Indian subcontinent is very impressive. Some of the works are on a vast scale, such as the Buddhas hewn *in situ* out of granite at Polonnaruwa, Sri Lanka. But artists were equally deft at working on an intricate scale,

Buddhist shrine *The Great Stupa of Sanchi dates originally from the 3rd century BC, and was built during the reign of King Asoka. The tumulus-like hemispherical structure is 53 ft (16 m) high and 131 ft (40 m) in diameter, and is surrounded by a stone balustrade with four gateways adorned with relief carvings depicting scenes from the life of the Buddha.*

as seen in the low relief carvings, saturated with detail, at the 6th-century AD temple to Vishnu at Dashavatara, Deogarh (Uttar Pradesh), depicting episodes from the *Ramayana*.

The Mauryan Empire (320-185 BC) was a highpoint for early Indian sculpture, as shown by the statues of a *yakshi* (nymph or nature deity) at Didargandj, near Patna, and of a *yaksha* (the male equivalent) in Patna itself. The voluptuousness of every curve of the body, the sensuality expressed in each roll of flesh, the polish of the stone and the precision of detail, the jewels and the cloth, impart an extraordinary grace and lightness-of-touch to these works.

Buddha and his 1000 images

The conversion to Buddhism of Emperor Asoka (269-232 BC) heralded a great flourish in Buddhist art. This was influenced initially by Greek and Persian styles, and later characterised by multiple images of the Buddha in temples. Stupas, housing sacred Buddhist relics, also became the focus of artistic creativity. Like many pre-historic monuments in Europe, they began as earth mounds but were later made more elaborate with stone cladding and sculpture. Buddhists, especially in the north, also developed a style of deeply symbolic paintings, of which *mandalas* and *tankas* are the best-known examples: detailed images on rolls of paper or cloth show gods and demons, saints and gurus, laid out according to strict rules to reflect the cosmic order.

Another golden age of Indian art was the Gupta Dynasty (319-*c.*550 AD), noted for its sculpture and for its painting, such as the wall-paintings in the caves at Ajanta. As part of the revival of Hinduism, Hindu art began to supplant Buddhist art, notably in northern India. The 11th-century temples of Khajuraho are richly endowed with tantric-style statues, featuring, most famously, dancers in erotic poses and scenes of love-making.

The delicacy of miniatures

Under the Mughals, creativity flourished across the whole spectrum of art. Painting came to the fore, in the form of miniatures. These were especially prized by Emperor Akbar, who founded a state workshop in Delhi where about 100 Hindu artists pursued their profession, working as teams under the direction of two Persian masters. When Akbar died in 1605, his library contained some 24 000 illuminated manuscripts. A page from a manuscript of the *Khamsa*, a collection of Persian poetry produced for Akbar in about 1595, is typical of this hybrid art. It represents an event in the life of Alexander the Great: he is immersed in the sea in a kind of glass diving-bell. The subject is treated as if it was contemporary and includes the depiction of several European figures. Its distinctive charm rests in the subtle coloration, the enthusiasm for detail, and the evocation of landscape.

After the Mughals' decline, miniature painting reached a further high point in 18th-century Pahari painting, from the Himalayan foothills to the north of Delhi. This was the last great manifestation of the Hindu artistic tradition before it was influenced by Western cultural traditions. Nonetheless, this cultural legacy has filtered through to the modern era with a number of leading contemporary artists, including the sculptor Anish Kapoor, the photographer Dayanita Singh, and painters Ganesh Pyne and Natvar Bhavsar.

Snake charmer Gandhara, an area around Peshawar in Pakistan, has yielded a wealth of Buddhist sculpture. This bodhisattva is clothed like a prince, with sacred thread, necklaces, earrings and a serpent headdress.

Khajuraho and the realm of senses

Khajuraho was once the capital of the Chandella Rajput dynasty, which flourished from the 9th to 13th centuries. After its decline, it was left to the jungle and remained unknown to the outside world for centuries. Neglect helped to preserve its extraordinary complex of 22 temples and the many thousands of sculptures that adorn the sacred sanctuaries and the temple walls. The gods are accompanied by their wives, servants, musicians, courtesans and heavenly dancers, the *apsaras*. Following the principles of tantric art, feminine beauty and energy is most celebrated here. Depicted with ample breasts, women are shown in poses designed to be pleasing to the gods. Whether bathing, combing their hair, stretching or offering uninhibited love, they display a sensual ease. No other work of art expresses eroticism on such a grand scale, or shows more explicitly the place given to sensuality and fecundity in the Hindu view of the Universe.

Eternal love Vishnu and his wife Lakshmi, depicted in stone at Khajuraho.

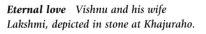

From shack to palace

Traditional dwellings on the subcontinent range from the simple modesty of a village shack to the extravagantly luxurious palaces of the maharajas. The biggest challenge is the climate: extremes of heat and damp gnaw away at even the grandest buildings. But traditional building methods, refined over centuries, fend off the worst conditions, and have been given a further twist by stylistic touches that reflect regional tastes, ethnicity and religion.

Natural materials *A house and courtyard built of earth and thatch in the Thar Desert of Rajasthan.*

The vast expanse of the subcontinent, the variety of climate and landscape, and several thousand years of history have created an extraordinary range of architectural expression. It is hard to find a common thread that runs from the shack of dried mud to the palace of the great Mughals in Agra, from the palm-thatched hut to the Jagannath temple at Puri in Orissa, except for the fact that all were built in the same country.

Individuality *Lavish artwork transforms a simple dwelling in Orissa.*

Wood and earth

Local materials have always dictated the form of ordinary dwellings. Relief carvings and paintings found on the earliest Buddhist monuments testify to the widespread use of thatch and wood in ancient times, and the use of wood remains common in regions where there are still woodlands and forests. These are usually areas of high rainfall, such as Nepal, Jammu and Kashmir, Himachal Pradesh, Assam and Kerala in India, and the Chittagong Hill Tracts in Bangladesh. Making a merit of their material, the window and door-frames are often profusely carved in these timber-rich regions.

No simpler form of dwelling could be devised than the windowless summer shelters of the Gujar nomadic herders in the western Himalayas, crudely but solidly built out of rock and earth, and

Organic growth *A house in the 'backwaters' of Kerala, made of materials found close at hand.*

roofed by turf resting on timber beams. In the inhospitable marshland of the Kutch region, in Gujarat, the traditional *bungas* are round houses with walls of clay and plaster on a wooden frame, and grass-thatched roofs. The inside walls are painted and decorated with tiny mirrors. In the desert regions of western Gujarat, Rajasthan and Sindh (over the border in Pakistan), most modest homes have mud walls and thatched roofs, but in the towns mud is used to create flat roofs.

Brick: heritage of the Indus Valley

Little remains of the buildings of the ancient Indus Valley civilisation apart from the most weatherproof materials, and the most prominent of these is brick. The skill of manufacturing brick was mastered some 5000 years ago, founding a legacy that India has exploited ever since. Another important legacy was urban planning. The neolithic site of Mehrgarh, which has been the focus of excavation for the past 30 years, is evidence of urban development dating back to the beginning of Indian history. The two capitals of the Indus Valley civilisation, Mohenjo-Daro and Harappa, were

Practical elegance *A mansion in Karaikudi (Chettinad), Tamil Nadu, reflects the wealth of its original owner, a 19th-century merchant.*

Hand-made *The wife of a Garo chief, from Meghalaya in north-eastern India, sits proudly in her home constructed entirely out of natural materials.*

131

built in brick and had advanced urban systems, such as underground sewers. Mohenjo-Daro was probably one of the largest cities of ancient times.

The earliest Hindu and Buddhist temples were no doubt built in ordinary perishable materials, such as wood and mud, but none of these have survived. However, during the last centuries BC, Hindu and Buddhist religious buildings were built of brick or stone, or carved straight out of rock. Some of the earliest surviving Buddhist temples and monasteries were cut out of the cliff-face, such as the famous caves of Ajanta, which date from the 3rd century BC to the 7th century AD. They were used to house monks during the rainy season.

The Dravidian *ratha* temples of southern India, such as the 7th-century Draupadi Ratha at Mahabalipuram, were also carved from rock, *in situ*. The form of many of these echoes peasant dwellings still found, for example, in Bengal today – square or rectangular constructions with walls made of planks or *pisé* (rammed earth or clay), covered by a thick thatch that rests on a timber frame radiating from a central crown. That this homely form was used as a temple structure is perfectly understandable: in India, a temple is a god's dwelling on Earth, the place where he or she is clothed and fed with offerings.

Crowning glory *The fortress of Amber in Rajasthan was begun in 1592.*

The quintessential Hindu temple

Most major Hindu temples are designed like symbolic maps of the Universe. Starting from the basis of the square (the perfect, pure shape), all within the temple has to conform to carefully planned proportions and positioning, dictated by ancient rules, as well as to astrological calculations. At the heart is the inner sanctum, the *garbhagriha*, where the god is said to reside. Above this rises the superstructure. This varies in form from the north of India (where it is called the *shikhara*) to the south (where it is called the *vimana*): both are said to imitate the archetypal Mountain of the Gods at the centre of the Earth, Mahameru, which supports the heavens. Walkways permit devotees to circumambulate (clockwise) the sacred centre, while scattered around the temple precinct (often walled) will be several lesser shrines. In the south, temples are usually fronted by long *mandapa*s (pillared pavilions), which provide

Cool view *The Hawa Mahal, or Palace of the Winds, in Jaipur, Rajasthan, was built in 1799. Women of the royal harem could sit in the cooling breeze behind stone screens and watch the activity in the street below.*

Masterwork *The Taj Mahal in Agra, built as a mausoleum between 1631 and 1653, involved 20 000 workers and craftsmen, including Italian specialists in stone inlay.*

access to the temple – a pattern that is followed from Ellora in Maharashtra to Mahabalipuram or Kanchipuram in Tamil Nadu.

Southern temple architecture reached a peak under the Pallava Dynasty (4th to 9th centuries), as seen in the magnificent 7th-century Shore Temple at Mahabalipuram, the inspiration for much of India's subsequent religious architecture. Ever larger and more lavishly decorated temples were built for the kings of the Chola dynasty in the 9th to 13th centuries, such as the temples of Dharasuram, Gangakondacholapuram and Tanjore (Thanjavur) – buildings whose pure outline shapes pulsate with sculptural detail.

The *havelis* of Shekhawati

The ornately decorated homes known as *havelis* are found particularly in Rajasthan and Gujarat. Few are more elegant than the merchants' houses in the isolated towns of the semi-desert Shekhawati region, in Rajasthan, built of cut stone from the 18th century on. A heavy wooden door leads into the first courtyard, where the walls are decorated with paintings and the doors are carved. This is repeated in the second courtyard, which includes rooms for the women, who, for religious reasons and security, lived in virtual seclusion. Generations of a single family would live in these houses in the past, but today many have been abandoned.

Artist's touch *Wall paintings in a haveli at Nawalgarh, Rajasthan.*

133

Muslim architecture in India

From the 9th to 14th centuries, a series of Islamic conquerors imposed their own architectural style upon the north of India, reflecting the religious zeal that inspired them. Derived largely from Persian precedents, Islamic shapes and details, such as domes and horseshoe arches, were applied to mosques, fortresses, palaces and tombs. Later, a synthesis between Muslim, Persian and Indian styles gave rise to the great Mughal buildings of Lahore, Agra and Delhi, many of them decorated with stone inlay.

Fatepur Sikri, near Agra, was the purpose-built capital of the Mughal Empire from 1571 to 1585, during part of the reign of Akbar. Containing a mosque, palaces, administrative buildings and audience chambers, it is the finest physical expression of the synthesis that the great emperor hoped to achieve between the various religions of his lands. Because of inadequate water supplies, the city was abandoned shortly after Akbar's death and became a ghost town, but it was almost perfectly preserved.

Of all the Mughal emperors, Shah Jahan (reigned 1628-58) made the greatest architectural impact. He was the inspiration behind Delhi's Red Fort and the Taj Mahal – considered by many to be the world's most beautiful building. A mausoleum to his favourite wife Mumtaz Mahal, the Taj Mahal is redolent with Islamic symbolism. The building itself is said to represent the throne of God, while the gardens, with four water channels, represent Paradise and its four rivers.

Anglo-Indian palaces

A lasting legacy of the Mughal era was the use of stone for civil architecture, which spread across the subcontinent; previously it had been used only for temples, and even palaces were made of wood and mud. Some of the most spectacular buildings of the north are the palaces built by the princes, either Hindu (raja, rana or maharaja) or Muslim (nawab). Built in the 19th or early 20th century, they often incorporate a mishmash of styles and foreign influences, but their extravagant scale, the profusion of ornament and the uninhibited use of colour make them unmistakably Indian.

A number of these palaces were originally fortresses, to which further buildings were added over the course of time. During the 19th century some palace complexes became as big as small towns, with 100 bedrooms, swimming pools, a theatre, ballrooms decorated in the style of a French

Privacy and ventilation Screens made of carved marble exhibit a typical Mughal blend of practicality and decorative flair.

château, and a stableyard full of carriages, or latterly, Rolls-Royces. After independence, princes were demoted to ordinary citizens, and many of their former palaces have been converted into hotels.

The bungalow, a colonial dream

The word bungalow describes a hybrid form of architecture that combined the humble *bangla* (house) of Bengal with the Victorian villa as interpreted by British India. The simplest bungalows had just two rooms, but others were vast mansions, sporting neoclassical adornments. More usually they were spacious and comfortable one-storey homes, focusing on a central reception room with bedrooms off the corridors leading through the two wings. A broad, covered verandah provided a cool, outdoor space and seating with shelter from the sun and rain.

The British also left a legacy of churches and imperial architecture. One of the most impressive is the Viceroy's House in New Delhi, built in the 1920s in the twilight of empire. Designed on a grand scale by Edwin Lutyens, it represents a succinct combination of European neoclassicism and the various historic Indian traditions of architecture. It is now the Rashtrapati Bhavan, the official residence of the president of India.

Artisans, in the service of the gods

In traditional Indian culture, there was never any meaningful distinction between art and crafts. Specialist craft workers produced wares to the highest standards, as religion and caste dictated. The same principle remains in operation today. Sacred rules about forms, proportions and colours still determine how craft products are made.

In the image of the gods *Clay is used to make idols, which play a central role in some religious festivals, notably the Durga Puja of Calcutta.*

The classical traditions of Indian arts and crafts developed around the temples and princely courts, to honour the gods. Although financed by the rich and powerful, it was the humble artisans who created the masterpieces, remaining anonymous, for they were doing no more than their sacred duty as laid down by their caste, in the service of their gods and their patrons.

Guardians of tradition

Traditionally, Indian artisans were villagers obliged to provide other castes with the products they required. The perfection to which they aspired in their work was rooted in the rules, scale and proportions which, it is said, were laid down by Vishvakarman, the 'Architect of the Universe' and the representative of supreme creative power. Even today, it is Vishvakarman who is invoked at the start of each working day. When asked the name of their caste, artisans will reply: 'I am Vishvakarman', as if to say: 'I do the work allocated to my varna; I am one with him whom I venerate, and to whom I submit when I work.' A master craftsman directs the work of several members of his caste, or simply of his family; he is the guardian of tradition, taking inspiration from the religious, symbolic and technical heritage that has been handed down to him by his elders.

Teamwork Bronze-workers put the finishing touches to newly cast images of the gods. They use ancient techniques of moulding, casting and shaping to make not only ritual objects but also domestic wares, such as water pots.

Bronze and gold

Indian metalworkers have been using the same techniques of smelting, moulding and shaping for several thousand years, but their techniques and effects vary from region to region. Among their key products are water pots made of copper and brass. These are prized objects, and a family's wealth can be measured by the

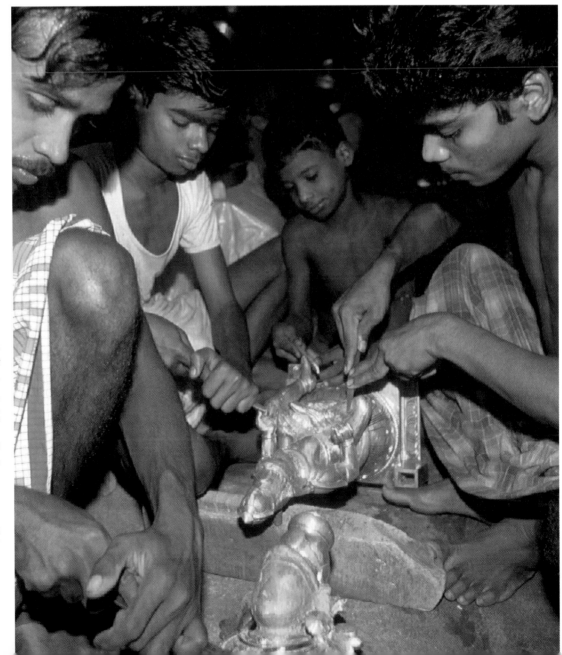

Decorative art In some regions, it is the women's task to decorate the home, a job to which they bring great flair and skill, as here in Mandawa, a town in Rajasthan.

number of water pots in their possession. Like the women's jewellery, these can be pawned in times of famine or sickness, or when some cash is needed to cover the cost of obligatory life-cycle rituals, notably the dowry of daughters.

Jewellery is made by gold-smiths, often seen hunched over their incandescent braziers, melting tiny quantities of gold in minuscule crucibles, before shaping their finished products with an array of rudimentary tools. Because of India's exceptional fondness for gold (it is the main form in which savings are held), and the need to provide jewellery as dowries for daughters, there are a great number of gold-smiths. For the well-off, marriage is an occasion to commission new necklaces, earrings and bracelets, or to rework old heirlooms.

The potters' wheel The ancient town of Bhaktapur in the Kathmandu Valley of Nepal has a potters' quarter.

For sale Pots at Kullu, in Himachal Pradesh.

Precious stones, enamels and pearls may also be added to these pieces: the jewellers of Rajasthan are particularly well-known for their jewel-encrusted designs.

Wood and stone

The traditions of sculpture and carving are closely linked to the Hindu temples. Communities of stonecutters and sculptors have grown up around the great religious buildings, such as those of Puri and Konark in Orissa, or Mahabalipuram in Tamil Nadu. Islam has likewise provided India with a rich heritage of ornate buildings, both religious (mosques, tombs) and civilian (pavilions, palaces), in which stone-workers have drawn on the traditions of Islam and Hinduism to create works of exceptionally delicate patterning.

Stonecutters also produce more mundane objects, although these are sometimes elegantly decorated, such as drinking troughs for farm animals, and mortars and pestles for crushing spices – indispensable items for the Indian kitchen.

Woodcarving is a particular speciality of Kashmir and Nepal. Local hardwoods are widely used to decorate the façades of houses and to make furniture. The Chettiar merchants of Karaikudi (Chettinad), in Tamil Nadu, who made their fortunes in Myanmar (Burma) in the 19th century, came home with cargoes of precious woods and had the timber decorated for use in their mansions by local wood-carvers.

Pottery and painted clay

Pottery goes back some 5000 years in India – or possibly further. Brahma, the creator god, is said to have made the human race from clay. Today, potters use a number of techniques: pots may be turned on the wheel, or worked by hand, or shaped in a mould.

The products cover the full range of goods: domestic bowls and utensils, ritual vessels, toys, decorative tiles and figurines, and even full-size statues of the gods created for annual festivals. In Tamil Nadu, temples dedicated to the village god, Ayannar, the guardian of the soil, are protected by soldiers and horses fashioned in a naïve style out of clay.

Weaving and embroidery

The weaver is said to symbolise the relationship between humankind and the cosmos: the 'Ordered Universe' is seen as a continuous piece of cloth, into whose mesh of warp and weft life – with all its cycles, illusions and dreams – is cast.

India is the land of cotton: it has cultivated, spun and woven it since the days of the Indus Valley civilisation and taught the world the techniques of cotton dyeing. Traditional cotton-production

Inlay A craftsman in Agra builds up a pattern by inserting small pieces of semi-precious stone in a disc of marble.

137

centres, often in close proximity to temples, had a latterday flourish during the 1960s, when all things Indian were in vogue in the Western world. More recently, Indian fashion has shown a reawakened interest in locally made, high-quality cotton goods. In a little village in Andhra Pradesh, 6000 weavers produce brushed and mercerised cotton of exceptionally fine quality for saris, and for export to the West. As for silk, this is thought to be the purest form of textile, and silkworms are farmed in a number of places.

The huge variety of designs and weaves reflects the breadth of knowledge and skills that have evolved in numerous regions or villages. Many of these production centres are famous for their sari cloth. Complex silk ikats called *patola*, for instance, are made in Patan in Gujarat, Pochampalli in Andhra Pradesh and in Orissa; Varanasi specialises in heavy silk brocades, while Bengal produces super-light muslins called *tangail*. Venkatgiri, from Andhra Pradesh, is a type of delicate cotton voile with gold-thread borders, while Chanderi in Madhya Pradesh makes brocades and muslins from cotton mixed with silk.

The art of the needle

Embroidery – the art of creating ornamental patterns on cloth using needles and coloured threads, in silk or cotton – has been practised in India since ancient times. The Western world has always been in awe of Indian skills in embroidery, and haute-couture fashion houses still use it to embellish their designs. In recent years, designers John Galliano and Jean-Paul Gaultier have both commissioned small workshops in Mumbai to produce embroidery for their couture collections. In Kashmir, skilled needleworkers create patterns of extraordinary harmony and subtlety on pashmina shawls. Some of these take as much as a year to produce, and duly command high prices.

Artisans and economic liberalisation

By some estimates, there are 10 million craft workers in India, 50 per cent of whom are hand-loom weavers. After independence, the Indian government put in place measures designed to protect craft workers from the economies of scale enjoyed by industry. But the liberalisation of the economy since 1991 has threatened to undermine the smaller producers. Villagers tend still to buy local goods, but competition from factory goods is driving down prices and hence the quality of craft products. This cycle of pressure is now threatening the very existence of craft workers throughout the country.

Fruit of the loom *A silk weaver in Varanasi operates his loom to produce a length of sari cloth.*

Spinning *Dyed wool is prepared for use in carpet-weaving.*

The women of Punjab produce *phulkari* (literally, 'flower-working'), a kind of embroidery using silk threads on thick, hand-woven cotton dyed with indigo or madder. *Chikan* is a famous product of Lucknow, in Uttar Pradesh: complex patterns are embroidered on white cotton muslin or voile. *Rumals*, made in the Chamba Valley of Himal Pradesh, are like pictures embroidered on patches of cotton voile: influenced by the Pahari school of miniature painting, they feature mythological scenes so neatly executed that they can be appreciated from both sides of the cloth.

The clothes of the nomadic herders of Rajasthan, the Kutch and Saurashtra in Gujarat are often decorated with mirrors and colourful motifs. Bags made to carry ordinary objects, curtains and other domestic textiles – even the cloth that is used to adorn cattle and horses – may be intricately decorated with this painstaking needlework.

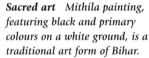

Sacred art *Mithila painting, featuring black and primary colours on a white ground, is a traditional art form of Bihar.*

Crafts showcase

The Crafts Museum of New Delhi was founded in 1956, and now has a collection of 20 000 exhibits, made of metal, wood, papier-mâché, clay, ivory and textiles. They include ancient as well as modern pieces, and thus bear witness to the long and continuing tradition of excellence that inspires the crafts of India today. The museum is housed in the Pragati Maidan Exhibition Grounds, to the east of the Rajpath, and forms part of a larger 'Village Life' complex. In the garden outside, craft workers demonstrate their skills and sell their products in a kind of village fair, while musicians and dancers perform to visitors. All these participants are selected by the museum authorities, and they work in rotation for stints of two weeks at a time. The museum also organises temporary exhibitions and conferences.

Needlework flowers *Women in Srinagar, capital of Indian Kashmir, apply their embroidery skills to their famous shawls.*

Maps, Facts and Figures

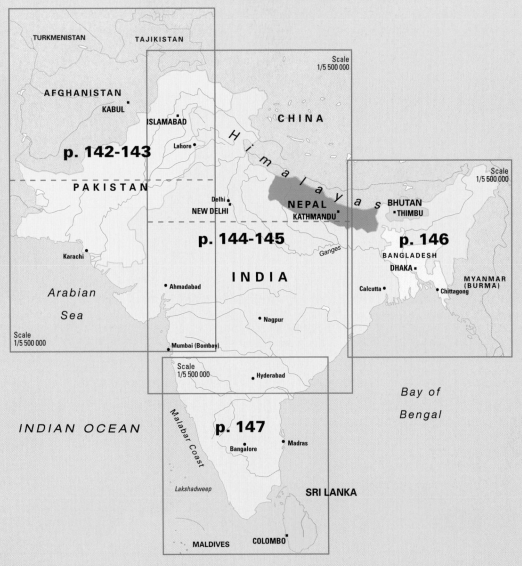

TURKMENISTAN
TAJIKISTAN

Scale
1/5 500 000

AFGHANISTAN
• KABUL

• ISLAMABAD

CHINA

p. 142-143

• Lahore

Himalayas

PAKISTAN

• Delhi
NEW DELHI

NEPAL
• KATHMANDU

BHUTAN
• THIMBU

Scale
1/5 500 000

p. 144-145

p. 146

• Karachi

Ganges

BANGLADESH
DHAKA •

MYANMAR
(BURMA)

INDIA

Calcutta •
• Chittagong

Arabian

Sea

• Ahmadabad

Scale
1/5 500 000

• Nagpur

Mumbai (Bombay) •

Scale
1/5 500 000

• Hyderabad

Bay of

Bengal

INDIAN OCEAN

Malabar Coast

p. 147

Bangalore •
• Madras

Lakshadweep

SRI LANKA

MALDIVES

COLOMBO •

Key to maps

Place names

■ **CAPITAL**   ● City

● Major city   • Town

Borders

——— International land frontier

- - - - - International maritime frontier

Topography

▲ Mt Everest
8848 m   Summit

HIMALAYAS   Mountain range

Elevation tints

Metres

8000
6000
4000
3000
2000
1000
500
0

Depth tints

Metres

- 200
- 500
- 1000
- 2000
- 3000

India (west) • Pakistan

KYRGYZSTAN
Fergana
Sary-Tash
Uch-Tyube
ALAI Mts
Lenin Peak 7 134 m
SARYKOL RANGE
Murghob
Murghob
Sarez
PAMIR
Kuli
Qullai Garmo (Communism Peak) 7 495 m
Qullai Revolyutsiya 6 987 m
Shadzud
Garm
Vanj
Khorough
Pyandzh
BADAKHSHAN
QATORKUHI ALICHURI JANUBI
Qullai-sep 7 010 m
Qullai-sep 7 016 m
WAKHAN
Wakhan
Langar
Nowshak 7 485 m
HINDU KUSH
Tirich Mir 7 690 m
Batura Wall 7 785 m
Baltit
Hunza
Rakaposhi 7 788 m
Gilgit
Gupis
Gilgit
Yasin
Ishkuman
Mastuj
Teru
Kalam
5 918 m
Swat
Chitral
Dir
Lashi
Feyzabad

TAJIKISTAN
DUSHANBE
Badzhuon
Kuybyshevskiy
Chakir
Konduz
Qonduz
Baghlan
Khanabad

UZBEKISTAN
Samarkand
Shakhrisabz
Karshi
Guzar
Karlyuk
Termez
Mukry
Andkhvoy
Sheberghan
Balkh
Mazar-e Sharif
Zari
Qizil

Kabul
KABUL
Kuh-e-Fuladi 5 143 m
Ghazni
Gardez

Chardzhev
Zerayshan
Pyandzh
Vaksh
Shirji
Harirud
Murghab
Qala Vali
Bala Morghab
Meymaneh

TURKMENISTAN
Karakum Desert
Mary
Zukhmet
Yolotan
Sandykachi
Kaoghan
Kaoghan

Balh
Shindand
Zarmardan
Dilaram

ASHGABAT
Tedzhen
Neyshabur
Quchan
Chanaran
Mashhad
Sarakhs
Torbat-e Jam
Torbat-e Heydariyeh
Ghurian
Herat
Farah

IRAN
Avaz
Bandan
Chakhansur
Khwaja Ali
Zaranj
Zabol
Zahedan
Zireh
Saindak
Nok Kundi
Ladiz

AFGHANISTAN
Malikdin
Kaloy
Ruhabad
Kandahar
Gereshk
Lashkar Gah
Poghdar
Goworan
Ahmad Wal
Koh-i-Maran

Registan
Dasht-i Margo
Gand-i-Zureh
Hamun-i-Lora
Helmand
Arghandab

PIR PANJAL RANGE
Nanga Parbat 8 126 m
Chilas
Bunji
Srinagar
Sopur
Baramula
Muzaffarabad
North West Frontier
Mansehra
Haripur
Abbottabad
Islamabad
ISLAMABAD
Rawalpindi
Wah
Attock
Campbellpore
Nowshera
Mardan
Charsadda
Peshawar
Khyber Pass 1 067 m
Kohat
Hangu
Thal
Bannu
Parachinar
Sadda
Jalai-Kut
Miram Shah
Wana
Zhob
Fort Sandeman
Kaloy
Tank
Kulachi
Darya Khan
Dera Isma'il Khan
Kalabagh
Isa Khel
Mianwali
Kundian
Pezu
Marabi
Darban
Gumal

Jhelum
Jammu
Sialkot
Gujrat
Gujranwala
Kamoke
Amritsar
Lahore
Ferozpur
Firozkot
Kapurthala
Faridkot
Muktsar
Fazilka
Pakpattan
Pathoki
Kasur
Okara
Sahiwal
Kamalia
Gojra
Samundri
Chiniot
Faisalabad
Jhang Maghiana
Jaranwala
Shekhupura
Hafizabad
Wazirabad
Bhera
Bahauddin
Mandi
Khushab
Sargodha
Rabwah
Talagang
Pindi Gheb
Gujar Khan
Chakwal
Mandra
Daud Khel
Mankera
Bhakkar
Karor
Leiah
Khanera
Khanewal
Muzaffargarh
Multan
Mandi Burewala
Harappa Road
Vihari
Vihari
Ravi
Chenab
Jhelum
Lala Musa
Thal
Desert

SULAIMAN RANGE
TOBA AND KAKAR RANGES
Takatu 2 964 m
3 485 m
3 277 m
Zhob
Kadanai
Ashewat
Murgha
Faqirzai
Ghazluna
Qam-ud-din Karez
Qila Abdullah
Chaman
Gulistan
Buri
Quetta
Mastung
Maran
Nushki
Duki
Harnai
Sanjawi
Ziarat
Pishin
Khanozai
Hindubagh
Mekhtar
Musa Khel Bazar
Kingri
Rokhni
Barkhan
Gomboli
Beji
Khost
Sibi
Nari
Bolan

Dera Ghazi Khan
Taunsa
Thok

142

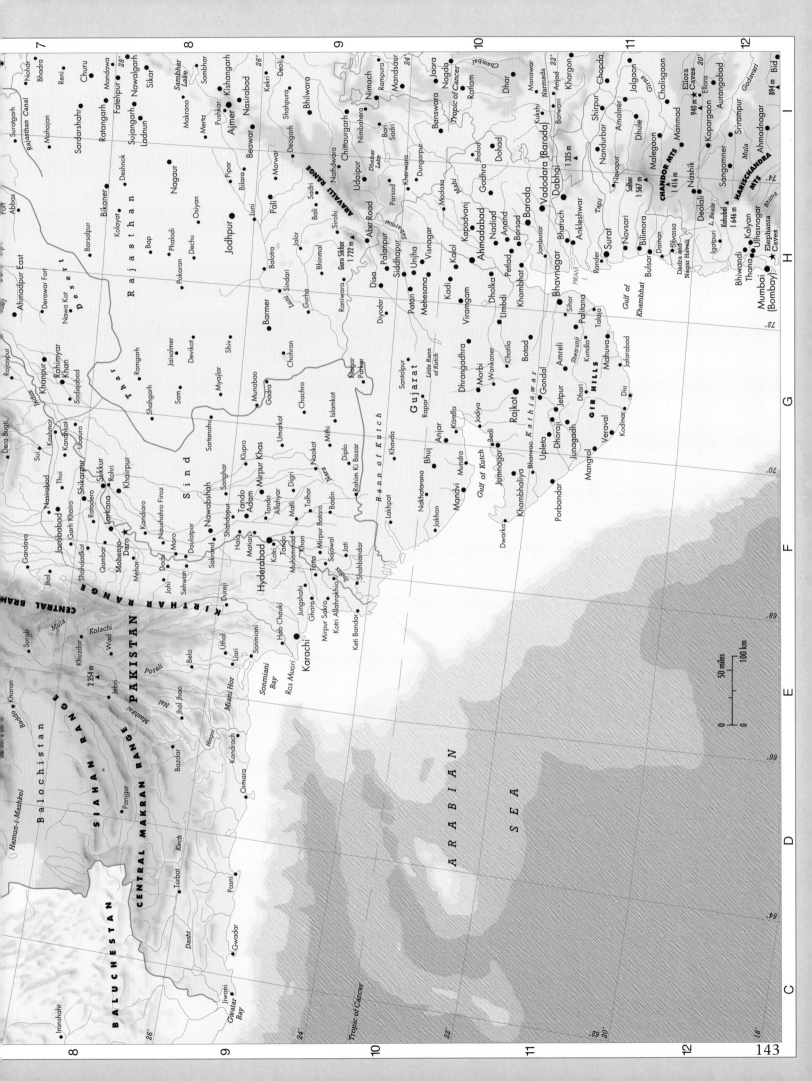

Qiemo · Darqahe · 6 303 m · Tuokusidawanling

Andirlangar · Karasay · KUNLUN SHAN

Minfeng · 6 626 m · Liushishan · Gahu Co

Xinjiang · Yutian · Pulu · 7 282 m · Muztag · Markham · Mange

CHINA

Taklimakan · Tarim Pendi

Moyu · Hotan · Lop · Qile · Bangdag Co · 6 401 m · Mawangkanlishan · 6 401 m · Lelishan · Lumajangdong Co

Zhaxi Co · Tongka Co · Zhari Namco · LABUCHONGSHAN · Bubuduo

Ngangla Ringco · Argu Co · Zhabuchakahu · Shifuhu · Meierkaisong

NGANGLONG KANGRI · Chabogongba · GANGDISE SHAN

Pishan · Keshitage · Xaidulla · Qizil Jilga · Haji Langar · Sumdo

Shangkasa · Rutog · Wujiang · Longka · Bakun · Dekamalu · Keerzong

Indus · 6 715 m · Gangdishan · Zhari

Barga · Barga · Niuke

Pulu · Takela · Yecheng · Yeerqianghe · Karakax He

Dafudar · Khunjerab Pass · 4 709 m · Kurakoram Pass 5 575 m · Chang Chenmo · Pangong Tso · Shyok · Hanle · Zhokixiang · Barga · Lagechi · Simikot

PAMIR · BADAKHSTAN · Chakir · Khorugh · Feyzabad

QATORKUHI ALICHURI JANUBI · VAKHAN · Darj ab se 7 010 m

HINDU KUSH · Mintaka Pass 4 755 m · 6 986 m

K2 (Godwin Austen) 8 611 m · KARAKORAM · Masherbrum · 7 821 m · Jammu · 7 788 m · Oisiaghil Sar.

Tirich Mir · 7 690 m · Chitral · 7 785 m · Batura Wall · Hunza 7 788 m · Rakaposhi · Gilgit · Skardu · Khapalu

SARYKOL RANGE · Sarhad · Ishkuman · Yasin · Ydsin · Gupis · Chilas

Nowshahr · 7 785 m · Mastuj · Dir · Saidu · Kalam · Swat

Khyber Pass 1 967 m · Peshawar · Charsadda · Campbellpore · Nowshera · Mardan · Mansehra · Abbotabad

Kohat · Pindi Gheb · Daud Khel · Talagang · Rawalpindi · ISLAMABAD · Haripur · Muzaffarabad

ZASKAR MTS · LADAKH RANGE · Leh · Upshi · Morari L. · 6 666 m · Zaskar · Padum · 6 517 m · Manali

KASHMIR · Kargil · Dras · Nunkun 7 135 m · Kishwar · 4 341 m · Chamba · Chini

DEOSAI MTS and · Burzil Pass 4 199 m · Anantnag · Udhampur

PIR PANJAL RANGE · Srinagar · Baramula · Sopur · Nanga Parbat 8 126 m · Bunji · Gilgit

Jammu · Kathua · Pathankot · Gurdaspur · Batala · Amritsar · Lahore

Himachal Pradesh · Mandi · Bilaspur · Shimla · L. Govind · Baas · Ambala

SIWALIK RANGE · Dehra Dun · Rishikesh · Nahan · Chakrata

MAHABHARAT · NEPAL · SIWALIK · Jumla · Dailekh · Sallyana

Annapurna 8 078 m · Dhaulagiri 8 172 m · Manaslu 8 156 m · KATHMANDU · Pokhara · Gurkha

Musiang · 7 043 m · 7 728 m · Api 7 132 m · 7 817 m · Nanda Devi · Kamet 7 156 m · Badrinath

Gyirong · Saga · Lage · Nawakot · Nuwakot · Kunchha · Bandipur · Butwal

Dhangarhi · BUDWA N.P. · Girwa · Jarakot · Siigarhi-Doti · Bajhang

KUNLUN SHAN

Gangotri · Chamoli · Joshimath · Almora · Ranikhet · Nainital

Ganges · Bajnath · Haldwani · Tanakpur · Pilibhit · Nepalganj · Nanpara

CORBETT NATIONAL PARK · Kashipur · Moradabad · Rampur · Bareilly

Najibabad · Bijnor · Amroha · Sambhal · Chandausi · Shahjahanpur

Roorkee · Deoband · Muzaffarnagar · Meerut · Hapur · Khurja · Aligarh · Kasganj

Saharanpur · Yamuna · Ghaziabad · NEW DELHI · Delhi · Gurgaon · Hodal

Karnal · Kaithal · Panipat · Sonipat · Rohtak · Rewari · Mahendragarh

HARYANA · Jind · Narwana · Hansi · Hisar · Bhiwani · Dadri · Nim Ka · Alwar

PUNJAB · Ludhiana · Khanna · Nabha · Patiala · Ambala · Chandigarh

Jullundur · Phagwara · Moga · Barnala · Sangrur · Sunam · Mansa · Sirsa

Hoshiarpur · Kapurthala · Jagraon · Kapura · Kot · Bathinda · Nohar · Bhadra

Ferozpur · Fazilka · Malaut · Muktsar · Faridkot · Abohar · Sri Ganganagar

Sialkot · Samba · Gujrat · Jhelum · Wazirabad · Gujranwala · Lahore · Kasur · Pattoki

Lala Musa · Gujar Khan · Mandra · Chakwal · Bhera · Mandi Bahauddin · Hafizabad

Chakwal · Khushab · Sargodha · Bhalwal · Shekhupura · Faisalabad · Chiniot · Jhang

Mianwali · Kundian · Khushab · Jhang Maghiana · Gojra · Kamalia · Samundri

Bannu · Isa Khel · Kalabagh · Monkera · Thal · Burewala · Vihari

Pezu · Lakki · Bhakkar · Karor · Leiah · Mandi Burewala

Dera Isma'il Khan · Darya Khan · Kot Addu · Muzaffargarh · Multan

PUNJAB · Khanewal · Kabirwala · Mailsi · Khanpur

Harappa Road · Sahiwal · Pakpattan · Arifwala · Chishtian · Bahawalnagar

Hangu · Thal · Kohat · Rabwah

Ravi · Chenab · Jhelum · Sutlej · Sutlej

Bahawalpur · Chishtian · Fort Abbas · Sri Ganganagar · Hanumangarh · Suratgarh

THAR · Thar · Rajasthan Canal · Bikaner · Mahajan · Kolayat

Naya Kot · Derawar Fort · Ahmadpur East · Barsalpur · Ratangarh

DESERT · Thar Desert · Rajasthan · Ladnun · Nawalgarh · Sujangarh · Churu

Deshnok · Nagaur · Sikar · Fatehpur · Mandawa

SHEKHAWATI · Chirawa · Loharu · Pilani

144

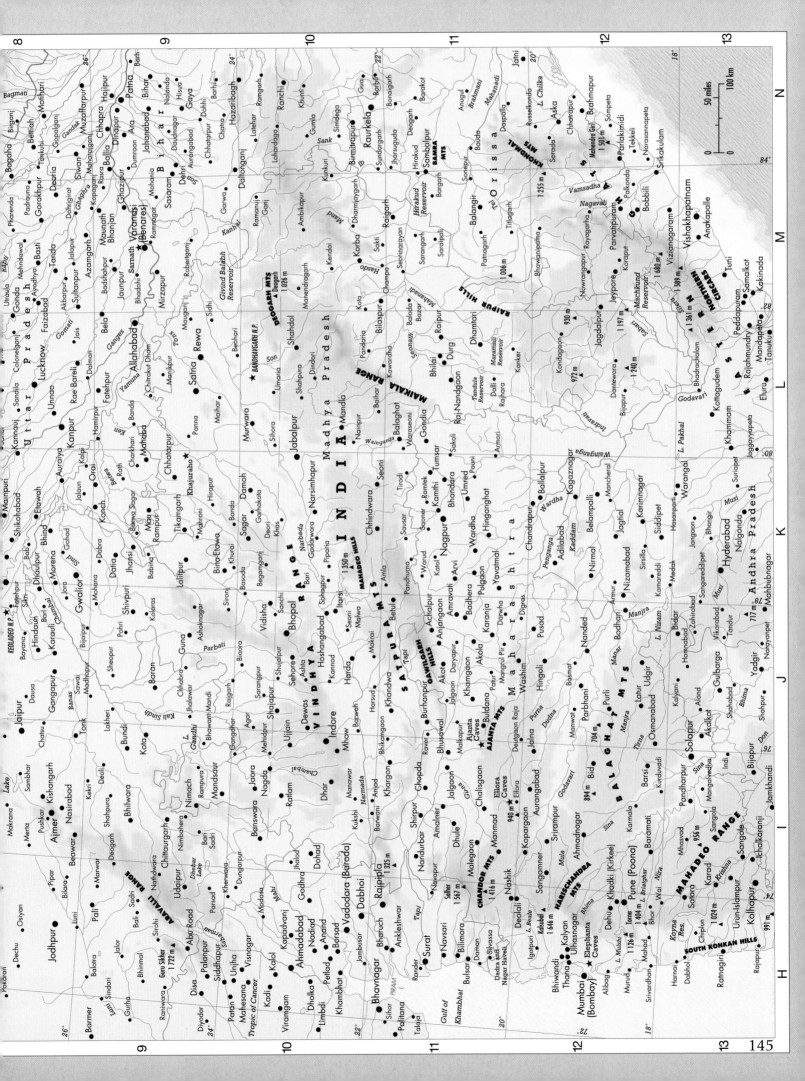

O P Q R S T

CHINA

Tangra
6 371 m
Keyangkeershan
Ngangzé Co
6 355 m
Telaopengshashan
5 716 m
Telumengtangshan
Shuru Co

Gyaring Co
Gomang Co
Bum Co
Xainza
Langmazong
Nam Co
7 088 m
Dangxiong
Jiali
Taizhao

T A N G H L A S H A N

7 755 m
Namuchabawashan

7 000 m
Gantanshan
Lhasa
Maizhokunggar

Goqen

Lage
Sangsang
Lingu
Xigaze (Shigatse)
Lhazê
Sa'gya
Gyangzê
7 252 m
Datong
Kangma
Chigu Co
Nedong
Yaguhu
Luozha
Lagangzong

Yarlung Zangbo (Brahmaputra)

M I S H M I M T S
Mipi
Chengele
Singing
Minutang
Hkakal

Yarlung Zangbo (Brahmaputra)

A r u n a c h a l
P r a d e s h
Mara
Riu
Pasighat
Sadiya
Luhit
Chonkham
4 578 m
Put

6 482 m
Qilagugannishan
Zuomuchedonghu
Gamba

7 038 m
Tingri
Cho Oyu
8 163 m
Makalu
8 481 m
7 145 m
Gauri Sankar
Mt Everest
8 848 m
8 598 m
Kanchenjunga
Chomo Lhari
7 314 m
Punakha
Wang du Phodrang
7 554 m
Kula Kangri
Lhuntsi Dzong
Tongsa Dzong
7 090 m
Kangta
Nyuri
Riang
Hachi
Ziro
Dibrugarh
Tinsukia
Dighoi
Margherita

S i k k i m
Gangtok
Kalimpong
Paro
THIMPHU
Chhukha Dzong
Trashigang Dzong

B H U T A N

I N D I A

Khowana
North Lakhimpur
Sibsagar
Nazira
P A T K A I R A N G E

Ramechhap
Okhaldhunga
Bhojpur
Dhankuta
Darjiling (Darjeeling)
Taplejing
S I W A L I K
N E P A L
Sirha
Udaypur
Dharan Bazar

Dalsingpara
Jayanti
Shiliguri
Mainaguri
Dhupgari
Koch Bihar
Alipur Duar

Bongaigaon
Barpeta
Goalpara
Nalbari
Mangaldai
Udalguri
Gohpur
Itanagar
Dergaon
Jorhat
Mariani
Mokokchung

Brahmaputra
Tezpur
KAZIRANGA N.P.
Mairabari
Nagaon
Golaghat
Barpathar

N a g a l a n d
Wokha

Madhubani
Nirmali
Supaul
Darbhanga
Biratnagar
Forbesganj
Araria
Kishanganj
Lalmanir Hat
Dinhata
Dhubri
South Salmara
Dudhnai
Dispur
Guwahati
Nakhola
Nongpoh
Hojai
Dimapur
Rajbari
Lumding
Langting
Kohima
Maram

A s s a m
Singkaling Hkamti
Myitkyina
Mogaung

Murliganj
Bihariganj
Purnia
Kasba
Saidpur
Dinajpur
Raiganj
Katihar
Parbatipur
Rangpur
Gaibanda
Hilli
Goalpara
Tura
Nongstoin
M e g h a l a y a
Shillong
Cherrapunji
Chhatak
Jaintrapur
Jowai
Haflong
Tamma
Kangpokpi
Ukhrul
Homalin
Katha
Bham

Baruni
Ganges
Munger
Mokama
Jamalpur
Bhagalpur
Shaikhpura
Jamui
Chakai
Banka
Sahibganj
Balurghat
Ingraj Bazar
Dhulian
Pakaur
Naogaon
Nawabganj
Nator
Bogra
Sirajganj
Sherpur
Jamalpur
Mymensingh
Netrakona
Kishorganj
Tangail
Sripur
Baniyachung
Habiganj
Khowai
Sylhet
Karimganj
Silchar
Lakhipur
Hailakandi
Bishenpur
Kulaura
Kusiyara
Jaria Jhanjail
M a n i p u r
Imphal
Logtak Lake

Giridih
Madhupur
Deoghar
Jangipur
Jiaganj
Rampur Hat
Baharampur
Kandi
I N D I A
Bokaro
Dhanbad
Asansol
Jaridih
Purulia
Raniganj
Durgapur
Burdwan
W e s t
B e n g a l
Bankura
Bishnupur
Katwa
Navadwip
Krishnagar
Santipur
Kalna
Ranaghat
Chakdaha
Damoca
Rajshahi
Ishurdi
Pabna
BANGLADESH
Kushtia
Chuadanga
Manikganj
Faridpur
Narayanganj
DHAKA (DACCA)
Brahmanbaria
Agartala
Comilla
T r i p u r a
Aizawl
Zopui
Sonamura
Belonia
M i z o r a m
Karnafuli Reservoir
Lunglei
Kalewa
M Y A N M A R (B U R M A)
Kalemyo
Falam
Ye-u
Shwebo
Tropic of Canc

Jamshedpur
Chaibasa
Ghatsila
Medinipur
Tamluk
Kharagpur
Haora
Baranagar
Kolkata (Calcutta)
Garden Reach
Diamond Harbour
Bhatpara
Jessore
Madaripur
Gopalganj
Khulna
Bagherhat
Piroipur
Barisal
Jhalakati
Feni
Laksham
Chandpur
Noakhali
Nazir Hat
Ramgarh
Rangamati
Kaptai
HATIA
SANDWIP
SOUTH HATIA ISLAND
M I Z O M T S
Barkal
C H I N H I L L S
Gangaw
Monywa
Mandalay
Amarapura
Maymyo

Jhargram
Baripada
Karanjia
Megasini
1 165 m
Baleshwar
Jaleshwar
Kanthi
Subarnarekha
Kakdwip
S u n d a r b a n s
Sundarbans National Park
Chittagong
Chandpur
Satkania
BANGLADESH
Reng Ilang 957 m
Chakaria
KUTUBDIA I.
Ramu
Paletwa
Pauk
Pakokku
Myingyan

Anandapur
Soro
Bhadrakh
Bhuban
Jajpur
Chandbali
M o u t h s o f t h e G a n g e s
MAISKHAL I.
Cox's Bazar
3 053 m
Mount Victoria
A R A K A N
Kyauktaw
Chauk
Meiktila
Thazi
Kal

Cuttack
Kendrapara
Jatni
Bhubaneshwar
Konarak
Puri

B a y o f B e n g a l

Sittwe (Akyab)
RAMREE ISLAND
CHEDUBA ISLAND
Kyaukpyu
Yenangyaung
Magwe
Pyinmana
Thayetmyo
Toungoo
Pyè
Paungde
Myanaung
Irrawaddy
Sittang

0   50 miles
0   50 100 km

O P Q R S

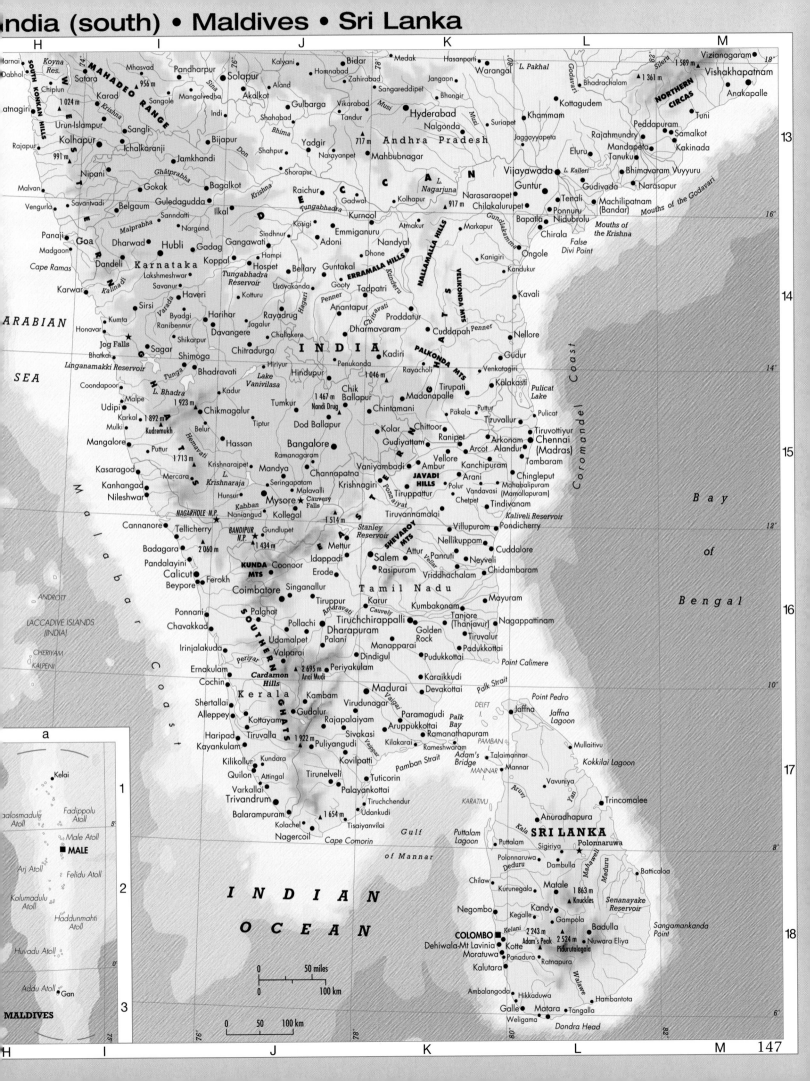

India and the countries of Southern Asia: the statistics

Southern Asia consists of a set of seven countries, neatly defined as a geographical mass, but forming a complex mosaic of ethnic, religious, linguistic and political differences. India is the giant among them, 'the world's largest democracy'; Bhutan, Sri Lanka and the Maldives are tiny by comparison.

PAKISTAN

BHUTAN

Official name: Kingdom of Bhutan
Capital: Thimphu
Area: 18 147sq miles (47 000 km²)
Population: 2 000 000
Population density: 110 per sq mile (43 per km²)
Ethnic composition: Bhotia 62.5%, Nepalese-Gurung 17.7%, Sherdukpen 13.2%, other 6.6%
Religions: Buddhist 75%, Hindu 25%
Currency: Ngultrum
GNP per head: $450
Languages: Dzongkha (official), Nepali
Government: Constitutional monarchy, assisted by a National Assembly
Flag (adopted in 1971): Saffron yellow (for royal power); red-orange (for Buddhist spiritual power); dragon (national symbol)

INDIA

Official name: Republic of India
Capital: New Delhi
Area: 1 269 213 sq miles (3 287 263 km²)
Population: 1 019 000 000
Population density: 803 per sq mile (310 per km²)
Ethnic composition: Very varied, but the four following groups dominate: Indo-Aryan, Dravidian, Sino-Tibetan, tribal groups
Religions: Hindu 82.5%, Muslim 11.5%, Christian 2.5%, Sikh 2%, Jain 0.5%
Currency: Rupee
GNP per head: $380
Languages: Hindi, English, Bengali, Assamese, Gujarati, Kannada (Kanarese), Kashmiri, Malayalam, Manipuri, Marathi, Nepali, Oriya, Punjabi, Sanskrit, Sindhi, Telugu, Urdu, Tamil
Government: Federal republic based on a multiparty system, with a parliament consisting of the House of the People (Lok Sabha) and the Council of States (Rajya Sabha)
Flag (adopted in 1947): Three horizontal bands of colour (saffron, white and green); on the white central band a blue wheel representing the chakra (Hindu or Buddhist wheel of life)

BANGLADESH

Official name: People's Republic of Bangladesh
Capital: Dhaka
Area: 55 597sq miles (143 998 km²)
Population: 123 000 000
Population density: 2212 per sq mile (854 per km²)
Ethnic composition: Bengali 98%, tribal groups (Chakma, Garo, Kuki, Mogh, Murang and others) 1.9%
Religions: Muslim 86.6% (Islam became state religion 1988); Hindu 12.1%, Buddhist 0.7%, Christian 0.6%
Currency: Taka
GNP per head: $250
Languages: Bengali (official), Urdu, Hindi, Sylheti, English
Government: Multi-party republic with a unicameral parliament
Flag (adopted in 1971): Green (representing fertility) with red disc (the struggle for freedom)

PAKISTAN

Official name: Islamic Republic of Pakistan
Capital: Islamabad
Area: 310 402 sq miles (803 943 km²)
Population: 148 166 000
Population density: 477 per sq mile (184 per km²)
Ethnic composition: Punjabi 48%, Pashtun 13%, Sindhi 12%, Saraiki 10%, Urdu 8%, others 9%
Religions: Islam 97%, others including Christian, Hindu, Buddhist 3%
Currency: Pakistani rupee
GNP per head: $455
Languages: Urdu (official), English
Government: In principle, an Islamic federal republic, with a multi-party system based on two legislative assemblies (Senate and National Assembly)
Flag (adopted in 1974): Green with Muslim white crescent and five-pointed star, with a white band representing other regions and minorities.

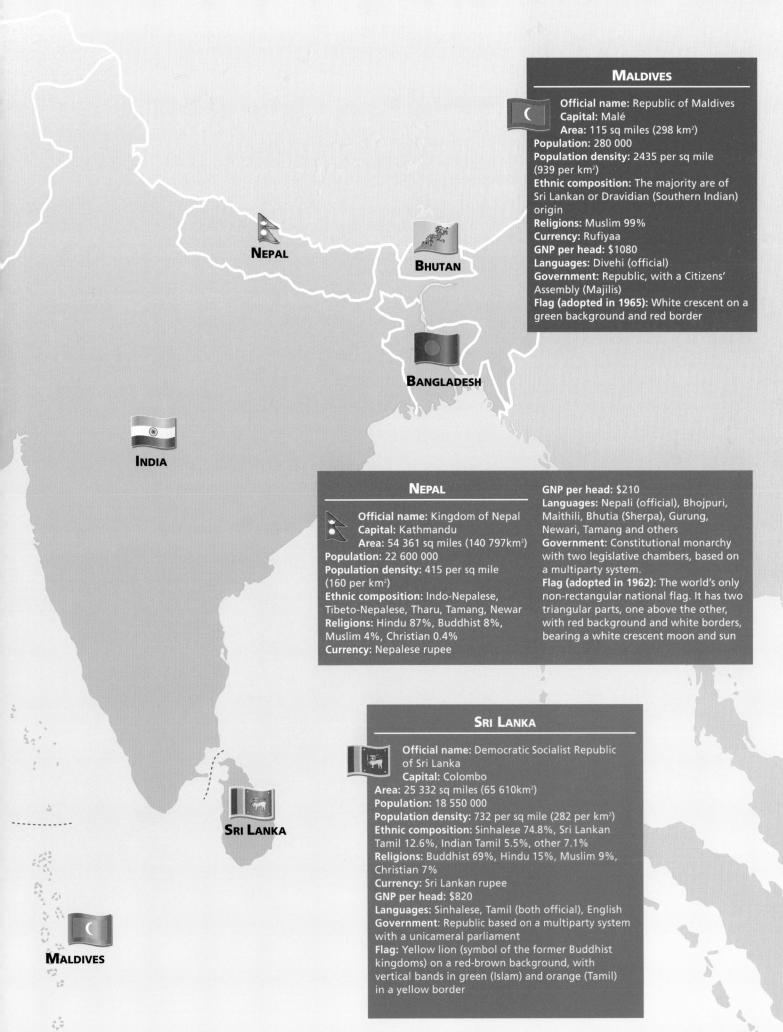

MALDIVES

Official name: Republic of Maldives
Capital: Malé
Area: 115 sq miles (298 km²)
Population: 280 000
Population density: 2435 per sq mile (939 per km²)
Ethnic composition: The majority are of Sri Lankan or Dravidian (Southern Indian) origin
Religions: Muslim 99%
Currency: Rufiyaa
GNP per head: $1080
Languages: Divehi (official)
Government: Republic, with a Citizens' Assembly (Majilis)
Flag (adopted in 1965): White crescent on a green background and red border

NEPAL

BHUTAN

BANGLADESH

INDIA

NEPAL

Official name: Kingdom of Nepal
Capital: Kathmandu
Area: 54 361 sq miles (140 797km²)
Population: 22 600 000
Population density: 415 per sq mile (160 per km²)
Ethnic composition: Indo-Nepalese, Tibeto-Nepalese, Tharu, Tamang, Newar
Religions: Hindu 87%, Buddhist 8%, Muslim 4%, Christian 0.4%
Currency: Nepalese rupee
GNP per head: $210
Languages: Nepali (official), Bhojpuri, Maithili, Bhutia (Sherpa), Gurung, Newari, Tamang and others
Government: Constitutional monarchy with two legislative chambers, based on a multiparty system.
Flag (adopted in 1962): The world's only non-rectangular national flag. It has two triangular parts, one above the other, with red background and white borders, bearing a white crescent moon and sun

SRI LANKA

Official name: Democratic Socialist Republic of Sri Lanka
Capital: Colombo
Area: 25 332 sq miles (65 610km²)
Population: 18 550 000
Population density: 732 per sq mile (282 per km²)
Ethnic composition: Sinhalese 74.8%, Sri Lankan Tamil 12.6%, Indian Tamil 5.5%, other 7.1%
Religions: Buddhist 69%, Hindu 15%, Muslim 9%, Christian 7%
Currency: Sri Lankan rupee
GNP per head: $820
Languages: Sinhalese, Tamil (both official), English
Government: Republic based on a multiparty system with a unicameral parliament
Flag: Yellow lion (symbol of the former Buddhist kingdoms) on a red-brown background, with vertical bands in green (Islam) and orange (Tamil) in a yellow border

SRI LANKA

MALDIVES

Climate and landscape

The Indian subcontinent, a vast triangle bordered in the north by the Himalayas, and rimmed in the south by the Indian Ocean, contains five countries: India, Pakistan, Bangladesh, Bhutan and Nepal. The island of Sri Lanka is separated from India by the narrow Palk Strait; to the south-west lies the long string of islands forming the Maldives.

Heat and humidity

The dominant feature of the Indian climate is the monsoon, which creates a dry winter (from November to May) and a wet summer (from June to September). Nepal, Bhutan and Bangladesh have a similar climatic pattern. India divides into the wetter parts (in the west, the Western Ghats; Kerala in the south; Assam and West Bengal in the northeast and drier parts (the inland Deccan; the northwest). Mawsynram in Meghalaya State is the world's wettest place, with 467 in (11 868 mm) of rain a year. Low-lying Bangladesh also has high rainfall during the monsoon. This can spell disaster, especially when heavy rains, coupled with the rivers in spate, coincide with hurricane-force cyclones that drive in across the Bay of Bengal.

The climate in the northwest is the driest in the region, producing the Thar Desert, and the arid landscape of Rajasthan. Much of Pakistan, up to the border with Afghanistan, is equally dry. Precipitation is low in the high reaches of the Himalayas, despite the snowy winters. Leh, the capital of Ladakh, receives 3.3 in (84 mm) a year.

In Sri Lanka, there are two monsoon seasons: it hits the south-west and central hill country from May to July; but it comes to the north from December to January. The climate of the Maldives is cooled constantly by sea-breezes, and a monsoon season from May to October brings daily rains.

RAINFALL (inches/mm)

	Total	Wettest month	Driest month
Dhaka	79.1 (2009)	Aug: 14.4 (365)	Jan: 0.5 (14)
Jaffna	52.2 (1328)	Nov: 16.1 (410)	June: 0.6 (16)
Jessore	63.2 (1605)	July: 12.4 (315)	Jan: 0.5 (14)
Kathmandu	56.1 (1424)	July: 14.8 (375)	Dec: 0.08 (2)
Lahore	19.5 (497)	Aug: 4.9 (125)	Nov: 0.1 (3)
Minicoy	63.7 (1618)	June: 11.6 (295)	Feb: 0.7 (18)
New Delhi	28.1 (713)	July: 8.3 (210)	Nov: 0.04 (1)
Peshawar	14.2 (361)	Mar: 2.6 (65)	June: 0.3 (7)
Srinagar	34.9 (886)	Mar: 4.1 (105)	Nov: 0.7 (18)

HOURS OF SUNSHINE (per year)

Dhaka	2546
Jaffna	2842
Jessore	2750
Kathmandu	2044
Lahore	3132
Minicoy	2256
New Delhi	2767
Peshawar	2919
Srinagar	2100

India: earthquake zone

On January 26, 2001 a dark cloud was cast over the 51st anniversary of the Indian Republic: a violent earthquake measuring 7.9 on the Richter scale shook the north-west of the country. It was the largest recorded in India for 50 years and was felt across northern India from Bombay to New Delhi, and even as far afield as Pakistan and Nepal. The state of Gujarat was the most severely affected, with about 20 000 people killed. The human agony was prolonged by the economic fallout. Gujarat was a centre for the textile industry, and had state-of-the-art factories producing chemicals, pharmaceuticals and electronic goods. These major sources of income have suffered from physical damage, loss of the workforce, and a decline in investment. Unfortunately, this will not be the last earthquake to strike the region: India lies on the edge of a tectonic plate that is advancing several inches every year and piling up the ridge that forms the Himalayas. Every now and then, these pressures will find release in another earthquake.

MEAN TEMPERATURES (°C/°F)

	January	July
Dhaka	19 (48.2)	29 (84.2)
Jaffna	25 (77)	29 (84.2)
Jessore	18 (64.4)	29 (84.2)
Kathmandu	8 (46.4)	25 (77)
Lahore	12 (53.6)	33 (91.4)
Minicoy	26 (78.8)	28 (82.4)
New Delhi	13 (55.4)	31 (87.8)
Peshawar	10 (50)	32 (89.6)
Srinagar	0 (32)	24 (75.2)

Devastation A major earthquake hit the state of Gujarat in January 2001.

Heading south   The Brahmaputra forms a broad river as it flows through Assam.

Landscape and land use

In Sri Lanka, as elsewhere in the subcontinent, climate and topography directly affect how the landscape is used, and hence what it looks like. The south is green with palm trees and rice fields, and forests and tea plantations at higher altitudes, while the flatter north is more arid.

Not much is left of the original natural vegetation of India: it was once thickly coated with monsoon forests of thorn trees and acacias, but these have gradually been stripped back for farming, and much of the land's natural fertility has been reduced by long-term overuse. Today, arid steppes cover much of the Deccan plateau and of the north-west. In large tracts of land bordering the Thar Desert, there is barely sufficient vegetation to graze sheep and goats. However, the starkness of such rain-starved regions is often tempered by irrigation-aided farming. This is the case in Pakistan, where irrigation turns the rich alluvial soils in the Indus basin and the valleys of its tributaries (all flowing out of the Himalayas) into highly productive farmland. In Bangladesh, the alluvial soils of the delta formed by the Ganges and the Brahmaputra are equally productive, but here the problem is not the lack of water, but an excess of it. Flooding is a constant problem, but considered a price worth paying for the copious crop yields.

The most productive farming area, however, is the Indo-Gangetic Plain, a former maritime gulf filled with sediments brought down from the mountains by powerful rivers, mainly the Indus and the Ganges. Indeed, this region, stretching from the Punjab to Bengal, is one of the most productive regions in the world, ranking second for its yield of rice, wheat and sugar.

RIVERS
(length in miles/km)

Ganges	1920 (3090)
Brahmaputra	1802 (2900)
Indus	1700 (2736)
Godavari	932 (1500)
Narmada	802 (1290)
Krishna	795 (1280)

FOREST COVER
(percentage of total area)

Bhutan	58.6
India	21.9
Nepal	35.2
Sri Lanka	27.8

HIGHEST PEAKS
(in feet/metres)

Everest (Nepal/China-Tibet)	29 029/8848
K2 (China/Pakistan)	28 251/8611
Kanchenjunga (Nepal/India)	28 169/8586
Lhotse (Nepal)	28 034/8545
Makalu (Nepal)	27 936/8515
Dhaulagiri (Nepal)	26 811/8172
Manaslu (Nepal)	26 758/8156
Nanga Parbat (Pakistan)	26 660/8126
Annapurna (Nepal)	26 545/8091

Peaks and valleys

The Himalayas have a generally temperate climate up to a height of 13 000 ft (4000 m). Up to that height they may be covered in forest: Bhutan has tropical forests in the south, yielding valuable woods, such as teak, sandalwood and rosewood. Above the tree-line, there are alpine meadows, then rock, snow and ice.

A relief map of Nepal shows bands of landscape running parallel from east to west. More than one-third of the country is covered by steep mountains and glaciers. In the far north, beyond the high valleys in the centre of the country, lie some of the highest peaks in the world, including Everest and Annapurna. But the fertile lowlands to the south drop away towards the Ganges Plain and benefit from the summer rains of the monsoon; here rice, sugar-cane and oranges are grown.

The Ghats – two ranges of hills and mountains that frame the Deccan peninsula – are hills by comparison. The Western Ghats, the source of all southern India's major rivers, rise to 3000-5000 ft (900-1500 m), while the Eastern Ghats are less tall at 1500-2000 ft (450-600 m).

Forest cover   Thick forest covers much of Arunachal Pradesh, in north-east India.

▲ **RELIEF MAP OF INDIA AND SOUTHERN ASIA**

Relief
height in metres

4000
2000
1000
500
200
0

First light   The peak of Everest catches the first golden light of dawn.

Population and economy

There are more than 1.3 billion people living in the Indian subcontinent – one-fifth of all humanity. In terms of standards of living, the disparities are considerable, but poverty and disposable wealth alone do not tell the whole story. The region has many of the largest cities in the world, but is primarily rural.

Health in India

At Independence in 1947, the state of health of most people in India was dire, exacerbated by basic inadequacies in hygiene, healthcare and clean water. Progress began to be made in the 1950s, especially in the cities. From 1955 to 1991, the number of faculties of medicine grew from 30 to 161. Plague and smallpox were eliminated in the mid-1970s. Malaria, which affected 75 million people in 1950, had all but disappeared by 1965. However, the curtailing of prevention programmes and mosquitoes' resistance to pesticides let it return, with a vengeance, during the 1980s. There are still some 3 million victims of leprosy in India and tuberculosis remains a major killer, despite vaccination campaigns. In the countryside, huge disparities prevail: there are villages with doctors and dispensing units, but many have none. There is still considerable work to be done and this accounts for a low life-expectancy in India; almost 20 years less than in countries with the highest life-expectancy, such as Japan.

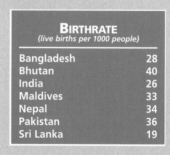

NATIONAL POPULATIONS	
(in millions)	
Bangladesh	123
Bhutan	2
India	1019
Maldives	0.3
Nepal	22.6
Pakistan	148.1
Sri Lanka	18.5

Population density
number of inhabitants/km²

- more than 200
- 100 to 200
- 40 to 100
- 10 to 40
- 2 to 10
- less than 2

POPULATION DENSITY ▲

INFANT MORTALITY	
(per 1000 live births)	
Bangladesh	79
Bhutan	63
India	72
Maldives	60
Nepal	84
Pakistan	74
Sri Lanka	18

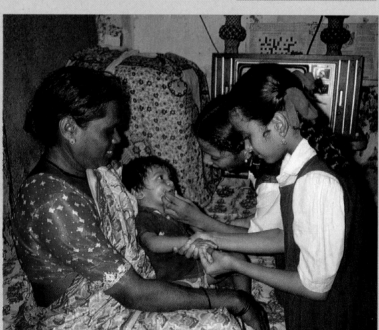

Learning to care Schoolgirls examine a baby in Mumbai (Bombay). Boys and girls are taught the basic principles of healthcare and hygiene at school from the ages of 11 to 14. Pupils then visit needy families (each child has two families to look after) and give them advice, which, for the greater part, is welcomed and heeded.

LIFE EXPECTANCY		
	Men	Women
Bangladesh	58	58
Bhutan	59	62
India	62	63
Maldives	65	62
Nepal	58	57
Pakistan	63	65
Sri Lanka	71	75

BIRTHRATE	
(live births per 1000 people)	
Bangladesh	28
Bhutan	40
India	26
Maldives	33
Nepal	34
Pakistan	36
Sri Lanka	19

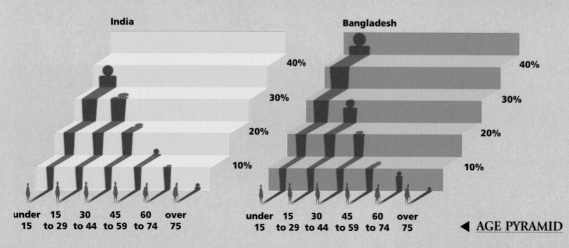

India / **Bangladesh**

under 15 / 15 to 29 / 30 to 44 / 45 to 59 / 60 to 74 / over 75

◀ **AGE PYRAMID**

FOREIGN TRADE OF INDIA, BANGLADESH AND SRI LANKA ▶

7042   3831

Bangladesh

42 201   32 881

India

5917   4732

Sri Lanka

Women in the subcontinent

The role of women in society varies greatly across the region, largely depending on traditional practices. In many parts of India, women have good access to education and to professions. They have freedom to conduct their lives as they please, except perhaps – and most notably – in marriage, where they are likely to be constrained by caste. That said, women from the poorer end of the social classes often have to carry out hard physical labour, in agriculture or construction.

In other parts of the subcontinent, women's lives are controlled by men. Because of fears of affronts to female honour, they are restricted to their homes, cannot go out without a chaperone, and can never meet or talk to any male in private who is not a relative, or visit public places of entertainment. This is particularly the case in some Muslim communities, notably in provincial Pakistan.

Despite the constraints in operation across the subcontinent, women have played a remarkably strong role in politics. Sirimavo Bandaranaike of Sri Lanka became the world's first woman prime minister in 1960; Indira Gandhi served as prime minister of India for 15 years. More surprising perhaps, given the conservative tendencies of Pakistani society, is the role that Benazir Bhutto (above) has played in her country. Daughter of the ousted prime minister Zulfikar Ali Bhutto, executed in 1979, she served as prime minister from 1988 to 1990 and 1993 to 1996.

Bhutan: an upward trend

This tiny Asian kingdom lies sandwiched between two major powers, China and India, on the rim of the Himalayas. It became a vassal state to British India in 1865, then a British protectorate in 1910, and an Indian protectorate in 1949; it has been independent since 1971. Since then, Bhutan has undergone development without suffering any of the great economic crises that have hit most of the continent. With a growth rate of 6% in recent years, since 1990 the country has doubled its gross domestic product (GDP) to $389 per capita per annum. This growth is explained in part by the construction of several hydroelectric dams, with six power stations and more planned. Increased production of timber, cement, coal, iron, copper and lead have also boosted the country's income. However, Bhutan still depends on substantial grants from India and, to a lesser extent, from the USA.

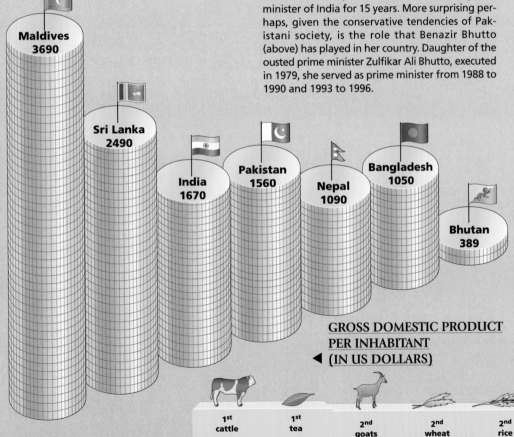

Maldives 3690

Sri Lanka 2490

India 1670

Pakistan 1560

Nepal 1090

Bangladesh 1050

Bhutan 389

GROSS DOMESTIC PRODUCT PER INHABITANT ◀ (IN US DOLLARS)

| 1st cattle | 1st tea | 2nd goats | 2nd wheat | 2nd rice | 2nd sugar cane | 3rd cotton | 3rd tobacco |

INDIA

KEY AGRICULTURAL ▶ PRODUCTS BY COUNTRY, WITH WORLD RANKING

3rd goats   4th cotton

PAKISTAN

4th rice

BANGLADESH

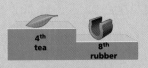

4th tea   8th rubber

SRI LANKA

5th buffaloes

NEPAL

The Maldives: the tourist archipelago

The Maldive Islands form a long chain stretching some 500 miles (820 km) from north to south. They include several thousand small coral islands (1192 are officially listed), grouped into 26 atolls. Only about 220 of the islands are inhabited. The sole urban centre is the capital, Malé. For more than two decades now, tourism has been the main source of revenue for the country. In contrast to the early 1970s, when just a handful of pioneer visitors came to the islands, the Maldives now receive more than 360 000 tourists a year – more than the total population of the islands. Some 90 per cent of these visitors spend two or three weeks on the islands, and tend to be big spenders.

The Maldives are solidly Islamic. To prevent contamination by Western values inimical to Islam, hotel development has been restricted to uninhabited islands. Contact between locals and tourists is limited and remains largely cordial. The government is aware that the nation has very few other resources besides fish: the bonito, a type of small tuna, is one of its few exports. The Maldives are therefore heavily dependent on tourism, but they prefer to see it develop slowly in order to remain its master, and not become its slave.

Riches of the sea The economy of the Maldives has been directed almost exclusively towards the sea: tourism and fishing are almost the only income-earners. Visitors revel in the coral sands, sun-filled skies and crystal-clear water, which is also much appreciated by scuba divers and snorkellers.

▲ URBANISATION
(as a percentage of the total population)

36	Pakistan
28 / 28	Maldives
23	India
20	Sri Lanka
11.3	Bangladesh
6.7	Nepal
	Bhutan

TOURIST VISITORS
(in 1996)

India	1 923 700
Nepal	404 400
Sri Lanka	366 000
Maldives	366 000
Pakistan	240 000
Bangladesh	157 000
Bhutan	5150

ILLITERACY ▶
(as a percentage of the adult population)

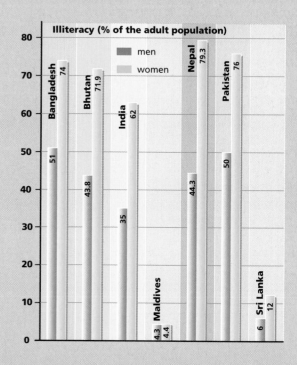

Illiteracy (% of the adult population)

- men
- women

	men	women
Bangladesh	51	74
Bhutan	43.8	71.9
India	35	62
Maldives	4.3	4.4
Nepal	44.3	79.3
Pakistan	50	76
Sri Lanka	6	12

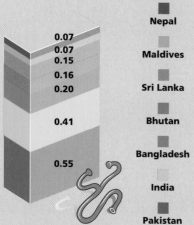

NUMBER OF DOCTORS
(per 1000 inhabitants)

0.07	Nepal
0.07 / 0.15	Maldives
0.16	Sri Lanka
0.20	Bhutan
0.41	Bangladesh
0.55	India
	Pakistan

MAJOR URBAN AREAS
(number of inhabitants)

Mumbai (Bombay)	14 600 000
Kolkata (Calcutta)	11 100 000
Karachi	9 700 000
Delhi	9 000 000
Dhaka	6 100 000
Chennai (Madras)	5 300 000
Bangalore	4 000 000
Lahore	3 000 000
Kanpur	2 500 000

Transport in India

An inheritance from the colonial era, India has a rail network with nearly 40 000 miles (64 000 km) of track, and a railway system that far outstrips those of the vast majority of developing countries. The efficiency of India's railways has been considerably improved in recent decades: single-track lines have been converted to double-track, and most of the major routes have been electrified. But these real signs of progress have not removed the continuing problem of serious bottlenecks at certain key points. Furthermore, passenger trains still travel fairly slowly over long distances. As a result, wealthier Indians and tourists often prefer to travel by air on internal flights, rather than take the train. Meanwhile, India's road network leaves much to be desired: many sections are too narrow, and there are virtually no motorways. Most secondary roads are not metalled. Such shortcomings in India's infrastructure have a knock-on effect on the economy as a whole.

Index

Page numbers in italics denote illustrations. The letter and number references in brackets are the co-ordinates for places in the map section, pp. 140-7.

155

Acknowledgements

Abbreviations: t = top, m = middle, b = bottom, l = left, r = right.

FRONT COVER: *View of the Golden Temple at Amritsar*: HOA QUI/X. Zimbardo.
BACK COVER: *Sorting cardamom pods*: CORBIS-SYGMA/Vo Treng Dung

4/5: HOA QUI/G. Rigoulet; 6/7: COSMOS/ SPL/J. Knighton; 8tl: ANA/R. Singh; 8/9: HOA QUI/M. Troncy; 9b: HOA QUI/Jouan-Rius; 10t: HOA QUI/V. Durruty; 10/11: DIAF/C. Senechal; 11t: ANA/G. Planchenault; 11b: DIAF/B. Morandi; 12/13: RAPHO/P. Koch; 13t: ASK IMAGES/J. Perrin; 13b: COSMOS/R. Frerck; 14/15: HOA QUI/B. Pérousse; 15t: DIAF/Pratt-Pries; 15b: RAPHO/M. Serrailler; 16l: CORBIS/Archivo Iconográfico; 16r: AKG PARIS/J.-L. Nou/Karachi, National Museum; 16/17: TOP/H. Champollion; 17m: BRIDGEMAN ART LIBRARY PARIS/National Museum of India, New Delhi; 17bl: AKG PARIS/J.-L. Nou/National Museum of India, New Delhi; 17br: HOA QUI/W. Buss; 18ml, m, b: BRIDGEMAN ART LIBRARY PARIS/National Museum of India, New Delhi; 18/19: CORBIS-SYGMA/D. Goupy; 19t, 20t: HOA QUI/W. Buss; 20b: BRIDGEMAN ART LIBRARY PARIS/British Library, London; 22b: HOA QUI/Ch. Boisvieux; 21t, b: AKG PARIS/J.-L. Nou; 22t: DIAF/B. Morandi; 22m: AKG PARIS/J.-L. Nou; 23t: HOA QUI/Ch. Boisvieux; 23m: BRIDGEMAN ART LIBRARY PARIS/National Museum of India, New Delhi; 23b, 24t: HOA QUI/Ch. Boisvieux; 24br: COSMOS/Robert-Bergerot; 24bl: HOA QUI/Ch. Boisvieux; 25bl: RMN/H. Lewandowski/Musée Guimet, Paris; 25br: AKG PARIS/W. Forman/Schatzkammer, Residenzmuseum, Munich; 26t: AKG PARIS/J.-L. Nou/Taj Mahal Museum, Agra; 26bl: RMN/Musée Guimet, Paris; 26br: RMN/Musée du Louvre, Paris; 27m: DIAF/B. Morandi; 27b: TOP/G. Sioen; 28t: BRIDGEMAN ART LIBRARY PARIS/British Library, London; 28bl: BRIDGEMAN ART LIBRARY PARIS/V & A Museum, London; 28br: DIAF/P. Cheuva; 29t: AKG PARIS/Archives P. Rübe; 29m: AFP/G. Duval; 29bl: ANA/R. Singh; 29br: AFP/J. Macdougall; 30/31: AFP/Raveendran; 32/33: DIAF/B. Morandi; 34t: HOA QUI/Jeon Hwasig; 34m: HOA QUI/Ph. Bourseiller; 34b: HOA QUI/F. Latreille; 34/35: HOA QUI/Jouan-Rius; 36t: AFP/D. Chowdhury; 36/37: ASK IMAGES/J. Perrin; 37t: AFP/D. Chowdhury; 37b: BLANC Jean-Charles; 38l: COSMOS/Impact/F. Lachenet; 38r: CORBIS/T. and G. Baldizzone; 39t: CORBIS-SYGMA/V. Miladinovic; 39b: CORBIS-SYGMA/Baldev; 40t: HOA QUI/Ph. Body; 40/41: HOA QUI/Globe Press; 41: HOA QUI/B. Pérousse; 42t: COSMOS/H. Aga; 42m: COSMOS/Robert-Bergerot; 42b: DIAF/P. Cheuva; 43t: HOA QUI/J. Horner; 43m: EXPLORER/J. Raga; 43b: SCOPE/M. Gotin; 44t: HOA QUI/Ch. Boisvieux; 44m: ANA/D. Ducoin; 44b: ANA/R. Charret; 45m: HOA QUI/M. Jozon; 45b: DIAF/B. Simmons; 46/47: CORBIS/L. Hebberd; 46bl: JACANA; 46br: BIOS/G. Martin; 47m: AFP/S. D'Souza; 47b: JACANA; 48/49: ANA/R. Singh; 50t: DIAF/J.-P. Garcin; 50b: SCOPE/M. Gotin; 51t: DIAF/G. Durand; 51m: COSMOS/M. Hemley; 51b: DIAF/L. Zylberman; 52m: SCOPE/Ch. Goupi; 52b: HOA QUI/X. Zimbardo; 53t: ANA/D. Ducoin; 53b: HOA QUI/S. Grandadam; 54t, b: CORBIS-SYGMA/Vo Treng Dung; 54m: COSMOS/Impact; 55t, b: CORBIS-SYGMA/Vo Treng Dung; 56t: RMN/Th. Ollivier/Musée Guimet, Paris; 56b: CORBIS/S. Collins; 57t: AFP/J. Eggitt; 57m: IMAPRESS/Camera Press; 57b: HOA QUI/JL. S. & S. E.; 58 t: AFP/I. Mukherjee; 58bl: CORBIS-SYGMA/Baldev; 58br: EXPLORER/R. Nickelsberg; 59t: COSMOS/D. Lainé; 59bl: HOA QUI/B. Pérousse;

59br: SCOPE/L. Audoubert; 60t: COSMOS/Robert-Bergerot; 60m: HOA QUI/B. Pérousse; 60b: ANA/M. Huteau; 61t: AFP/H. Mata; 61m: CORBIS-SYGMA/R. F. Smith; 61b: AFP/F Guillot; 62t: AKG PARIS/Archives P. Rühe; 62m: CORBIS/L. Aigner; 62/63: CORBIS/R. Ergenbright; 63t: CORBIS-SYGMA/Derimais; 63m: GAMMA/G. Saussier; 64/65: COSMOS/Katz Pictures/D. Beatty; 66l: CORBIS-SYGMA/D. Goupy; 66/67: HOA QUI/Ch. Boisvieux; 67tl: GAMMA/Bartholomew; 67tr: AFP/D. E. Curran; 68t: CORBIS/R. Holmes; 68b: SCOPE/A. Jongen; 69t: DIAF/P. Cheuva; 69b: CORBIS/J. Horner; 70t: RMN/H. Lewandowski/Musée Guimet, Paris; 70b: AFP/Raveendran; 71t: HOA QUI/Ch. Boisvieux; 71m: TOP/F. Ancellet; 71b: GAMMA/Ch. Boisvieux; 72bl: AFP/S. D'Souza; 72br: GAMMA/E. Bouvet; 73t: ANA/M. Borchi; 73r: HOA QUI/X. Zimbardo; 73bl: HOA QUI/V. Durruty; 74t: RAPHO/R. and S. Michaud; 74b: CORBIS-SYGMA/Baldev; 75t: ANA/L. Taylor; 75m: HOA QUI/Ch. Boisvieux; 75b: ANA/J.-C. Fauchon; 76t: SCOPE/M. Gotin; 76/77: HOA QUI/Ch. Boisvieux; 77t: EXPLORER/Raga; 77m: AKG PARIS/J.-L. Nou/National Museum, Colombo; 78t: HOA QUI/Ch. Boisvieux; 78b: HOA QUI/P. de Wilde; 79t, b: CORBIS/L. Hebberd; 79m: CORBIS/T. Streshinsky; 80t: DIAF/B. Morandi; 80bl: HOA QUI/Ch. Boisvieux; 80br: CORBIS-SYGMA/Baldev; 81t: ASK IMAGES/J. Perrin; 81m: COSMOS/Robert-Bergerot; 81b: GAMMA/E. Bouvet; 82t: CORBIS/E. and N. Kowall; 82b: DIAF/B. Morandi; 83t: HOA QUI/X. Zimbardo; 83bl: DIAF/M. Schoenahl; 83br: CORBIS/L. Hebberd; 84t: HOA QUI/J. Horner; 84m: DIAF/Valdin; 84b: DIAF/J.-Ch. Pironon; 85m: J.-Ch. BLANC ; 85b: DIAF/J.-Ch. Pironon; 86t: SCOPE/Ch. Goupi; 86m: EXPLORER/Giraudon; 86b: AFP/Arko Datta; 87t: COSMOS/Material World/P. Ginter; 87bl: HOA QUI/Ch. Boisvieux; 87br: HOA QUI/X. Zimbardo; 88m: HOA QUI/B. Pérousse; 88b: HOA QUI/V. Durruty; 89t: BLANC Jean-Charles; 89m: CORBIS-SYGMA/F. Soltan; 89b: CORBIS-SYGMA/S. Savolainen; 90t: HOA QUI/A. Wright; 90b: DIAF/B. Morandi; 91t: CORBIS/C. Karnow; 91b: GAMMA/J. Klatchko; 92m: ASK IMAGES/J. Perrin; 92b: CORBIS-SYGMA/M. Philippot; 92/93: CORBIS-SYGMA/I. Dean; 93t: CORBIS/J. Horner; 93m: CORBIS-SYGMA/Baldev; 93b: CORBIS/Bettmann; 94/95: ASK IMAGES/L. Weyl; 96t: CORBIS-SYGMA/Ch. Simonpietri; 96b: CORBIS-SYGMA/F. Soltan; 97t: DIAF/A. Even; 97m: COSMOS/Robert-Bergerot; 97bl: CORBIS-SYGMA/F. Soltan; 97br: CORBIS/W. Forman; 98/103: ANA/J. Ducoin; 98t: HOA QUI/P. de Wilde; 98b: ASK IMAGES/J. Perrin; 99t: EXPLORER/R. Mattes; 99bl: EXPLORER/Geopress; 99br: HOA QUI/Ch. Boisvieux; 100t: COSMOS/Impact Visuals/C. Villalion; 100b: HOA QUI/Ch. Boisvieux; 101tl: CORBIS/J. Horner; 101tr: ASK IMAGES/L. Weyl; 101ml: HOA QUI/Ch. Boisvieux; 101mr: HOA QUI/B. Pérousse; 101bl: TOP/A. Petit; 101br, 102tl: ANA/R. Singh; 101r: ANA/J. Ducoin; 102ml: TOP/G. Sioen; 102mr, bl: HOA QUI/Ch. Boisvieux; 102br: ANA/R. Singh; 103t: HOA QUI/Ch. Boisvieux; 103m: GAMMA/E. Martin; 103b: EXPLORER/R. Mattes; 104t: CORBIS-SYGMA/Ch. Simonpietri; 104b: EXPLORER/R. Nickelsberg; 105t: HOA QUI/B. Pérousse, 105m: HOA QUI/F. Charel; 105b: CORBIS-SYGMA/F. Soltan; 106t: HOA QUI/Ch. Boisvieux; 106m: CORBIS/MIT Collection; 106b: EXPLORER/F. Arvidsson; 107t: CORBIS-SYGMA/Baldev; 107b: CORBIS-SYGMA/D. Aubert; 108/109: HOA QUI/A. Wright; 108m: HOA QUI/Ph. Bod; 108b: HOA QUI/Ch. Boisvieux; 109:

EXPLORER/G. Boutin; 110t: GAMMA/Freedman; 110m: EXPLORER/Ch. Boisvieux; 110b: AFP/J. Macdougall/ Le Corbusier © FLC, ADAGP, Paris 2001; 111t: HOA QUI/G. Boutin; 111bl: CORBIS/J. Horner; 111br: CORBIS/Travel Ink; 112m: DIAF/G. Durand; 112b: COSMOS/M. Hemley; 112/113: DIAF/Ifa Bilderteam; 113t: HOA QUI/J.-L. Dugast; 113b: DIAF/J.-Ch. Pironon; 114/115: EXPLORER/Ch. Boisvieux; 116t: SCOPE/A. Jongen; 116b: ANA/R. Singh; 117t, b: HOA QUI/X. Zimbardo; 118t: HOA QUI/C. & J. Lénars; 118bl: COSMOS/Robert-Bergerot; 118ml, mb: RAPHO/Soldeville; 118/119: GAMMA/G. Smith; 119r: AFP/S. D'Souza; 120t: GAMMA/Bartholome; 120b: RMN/Arnaudet/Musée Guimet, Paris; 120/121: AFP/S. D'Souza; 121t: HOA QUI/X. Zimbardo; 121b: DIAF/B. Morandi; 122t: COSMOS/Robert-Bergerot; 122bl: ANA/M. Huteau; 122/123: HOA QUI/X. Zimbardo; 123: CORBIS/R. Holmes; 124/125: AKG PARIS/J.-L. Nou/Bharat Kala Bhawan Museum, Varanasi; 124bm: BRIDGEMAN ART LIBRARY PARIS/Dinodia Picture Agency; 124br: AKG PARIS; 125t: GAMMA/F. Reglain; 125bl: AFP/J. Macdougall; 125br: AFP/TekeeTanwar; 126t: GAMMA/Spooner; 126b: GAMMA/Bartholomew; 127ml: HOA QUI/Ch. Boisvieux; 127tr: AFP/D. Chowdhury; 127b: CORBIS-SYGMA/J. Van Hasselt; 128t: RMN/Musée Guimet, Paris; 128m, b: AKG PARIS/J.-L. Nou; 129m: AKG PARIS/E. Lessing; 129b: HOA QUI/P. de Wilde; 130t: SCOPE/P. Desclos; 130bl: HOA QUI/V. Durruty; 130/131: CORBIS/E. and N. Kowall; 131t: DIAF/P. Cheuva; 131b: HOA QUI/N. Thibaut; 132/133t: EXPLORER/Geopress; 132/133b: DIAF/P. Cheuva; 133t: ANA/M. Durazzo; 133b: HOA QUI/B. Pérousse; 134: ANA/M. Durazzo; 135t: HOA QUI/X. Zimbardo; 135b: CORBIS-SYGMA/F. Soltan; 136t: HOA QUI/V. Durruty; 136b: ANA/Henneghien; 137bl: HOA QUI/X. Zimbardo; 137br: ANA/M. Borchi; 138t: CORBIS/L. Hebberd; 138b: EXPLORER/R. Harding Pict. Lib./J. H. C. Wilson; 139t: HOA QUI/X. Zimbardo; 139b: CORBIS/L. Hebberd; 140/141: EXPLORER/R. Harding Pict. Lib./A. Woolfitt; 150: CORBIS-SYGMA/Baldev; 151t: RAPHO/S. and R. Michaud; 151m: HOA QUI/X. Zimbardo; 151b: DIAF/B. Coleman; 152: CORBIS-SYGMA/F. Soltan; 153: CORBIS-SYGMA; 154: HOA QUI/B. Pérousse.

Printing and binding: Printer Industria Gráfica S.A., Barcelona
Colour separations: Station Graphique, Ivry-sur-Seine

617-016-01